Contents

Preface   ix

1   Learning from Other Countries:
Current Benefits and Future Opportunities   1

2   Policies and Programs in Aging:
International Initiatives   13

3   Exploring Child Welfare through
International Innovations   31

4   Individual Retirement Accounts,
Privatization and Social Security:
International Experiences   53

5   Welfare, Poverty and Social Services:
International Experiences   75

6   Mental Health Lessons from Abroad   93

7   Social Development: Lessons from
the Global South   117

8   International Social Welfare
Treaties and Conventions:
Implications for the United States   137

Index   159

About the Editors   165

Lessons from Abroad

Lessons from Abroad
Adapting International
Social Welfare Innovations

EDITED BY
M.C. Hokenstad
and
James Midgley

NASW PRESS

Gary Bailey, MSW, *President*
Elizabeth J. Clark, PhD, ACSW, MPH, *Executive Director*
Cheryl Y. Bradley, *Publisher*
Paula L. Delo, *Executive Editor*
Heather Brady, *Editor*
Leonard Rosenbaum, *Indexer*

Cover by Cohen Design
Interior design by Electronic Quill
Printed and bound by Port City Press

Library of Congress Cataloging-in-Publication Data

Lessons from abroad : adapting international social welfare innovations / edited by M. C. Hokenstad, James Midgley.
    p. cm.
  Includes bibliographical references and index.
  ISBN 0-87101-360-6
  1. Human services—Case studies. 2. Social services—Case studies. 3. Social security—Case studies. 4. Community development—Case studies. 5. Human services—United States. 6. Social service—United States. 7. Human services—International cooperation. 8. Social service—International cooperation. I. Hokenstad, Merl C. II. Midgley, James. III. National Association of Social Workers.
  HV40.L45 2004
  361.2'5—dc22   2004007996

Printed in the United States of America

Dedication

To my wife Dorothy with thanks for welcoming hundreds of international friends, colleagues, and students into our home over these many years.

M.C. Hokenstad

To my former international students, and many international colleagues and friends who have taught me many "lessons from abroad."

James Midgley

Preface

International exchanges in social work can be traced back to the earliest years of the profession's history. In the 19ᵗʰ century, innovations in social work practice diffused from European countries such as Britain to the United States, and later, American approaches were adopted in Europe and elsewhere. However, exchanges between social workers in different countries occurred in a rather haphazard way and the question of whether the international adoption of innovations was appropriate to local cultural, social or economic realities was not always carefully considered. This resulted in the accusation that exchanges were often unilateral and unsuited to other nations. During the post-World War II decades, as social work expanded in the developing countries, the practice of adopting social work approaches from the industrial nations was hotly debated and the need for a more discerning attitude to the diffusion of innovations was emphasized. Although diverse views on this issue have been expressed, it is today generally accepted that mutuality and the reciprocal sharing of social work knowledge and practice approaches should characterize international exchanges in social work. This implies that social workers in all parts of the world can learn from each other.

In this context, this book presents a number of case examples of how innovations in other countries can inform social work and social welfare in the United States. Although social workers in the United States are regarded as among the world's leaders in formulating innovative approaches to social work and social welfare, we believe that social workers and social welfare policymakers in the United states have much to learn from colleagues in other nations. Indeed, we take the position that no matter how well developed or tested practice and policy approaches may be, there are always opportunities to share experiences and learn from others. This belief has motivated us to commission a series of chapters for this collection that offer examples of how domestic policies and practices in social work and social welfare can be enhanced by documenting, analyzing and judiciously adapting approaches emanating from other countries. Despite significant differences in culture, social conditions, levels of economic development, and political institutions, the nations of the world share a common humanity which is conducive to collaboration in the cause of promoting the well-being of all. At a time when divisive global forces have become increasingly influential, this book seeks to demonstrate in a small way that collaboration is possible and that we can benefit from mutual exchanges with our colleagues in other parts of the world.

This book is the third in a series of NASW publications which we have been fortunate to edit. Together with our colleague, Shanti Khinduka, we compiled one of the first systematic accounts of professional social work around the world. *Profiles in International Social Work* (NASW Press, 1992) presented case studies of the way the social work profession was organized in different nations and of the challenges it faced. This publication was followed by *Issues in International Social Work* (NASW Press, 1997), which focused on social work's involvement with a number of internationally pressing issues ranging from the refugee crisis to the AIDS pandemic. This third book, *Lessons from Abroad: Adapting International Social Welfare Innovations*, is concerned with the adaptation of international innovations to inform social work practice and in social welfare policy in the United States. We hope that this book will stimulate further discussion of how we in the United States can learn from the experiences in other countries, and how these experiences can inform our own policies and practice innovations.

The publication of this book coincides with a growing interest in international social work. Although, as noted earlier, international exchanges in social work are hardly new, international collaboration was previously regarded as an exotic activity undertaken by specialists who had lived abroad or who had special knowledge of professional activities of other nations. The more frequent publications of articles and books on international social work and a heightened interest in international issues at social work conferences and meetings are reflective of a wider interest in the subject among social work practitioners. It also reflects the increasing contacts that are taking place between social workers in different parts of the world. This book hopes to show that purposeful collaboration that results in the considered adaption of innovations from around the world can promote social work's global relevance and further its goals.

We are grateful to NASW Press for publishing this book and particularly to Paula Delo, Executive Editor, and Steph Selice, Senior Editor for their support and confidence in this project. We would also like to thank NASW's Publications Committee under the former leadership of Shanti Khinduka and Nazneen Mayadas, and now Leslie Leighninger, for their encouragement. Thanks to editor Heather Brady, Staff Editor, for seeing the project through to production and for a very high standard of copyediting. Special thanks are due to our contributors who not only adapted their own ideas to fit the editorial requirements of the book but congenially met deadlines and other requests. The book would not have made the transition from concept to reality without their cooperation and dedication. Theresa Lydonne Wilson at Case Western Reserve University and Maureen Hogan at Berkeley provided willing and indispensable support. They ensured that the numerous editorial and secretarial tasks a project of this kind involves were efficiently undertaken.

M.C. Hokenstad
Case Western Reserve University
Cleveland, Ohio

James Midgley
University of California
Berkeley

CHAPTER ONE

Lessons from Other Countries: Current Benefits and Future Opportunities

M.C. Hokenstad AND James Midgley

Global interdependence is a reality of the 21st century. Economic and social interdependence are now equally important to political interdependence. Globalization became the dominant economic system at the end of the last century, and now is a major determinant of domestic politics as well as international relations. Friedman (2000) documents in depth how it now shapes the lives of nations, organizations, and individuals throughout the world. Opportunities for rapid exchange of information and ideas through telecommunications technology provide daily reminders of global interdependence.

While this system creates opportunities for improved quality of life, it also creates and accentuates social problems. Structural unemployment due to world trade policies affects tens of millions in many countries, including the United States. The international drug trade is a major contributor to drug addiction. The HIV virus spreads throughout the world, making AIDS a global problem. Poverty resulting from international debt and a growing number of refugees resulting from ethnic and religious conflict are other major social problems of the 21st century with international agents and impact.

Events at the beginning of the new millennium have shocked Americans into recognizing the dark side of global interaction. The tragedy

1

of September 11, 2001, brought home the reality that what is happening in the rest of the world can have a direct impact on the United States and the citizens of this country. The U.S. is a geographically insulated, demographically diverse, and politically powerful nation. For these and other reasons, its policies reflect a curious blend of internationalism and isolationism. The terror of 9/11 was a wake-up call: No nation can ignore international interdependence in the 21st century. This nation's interaction with both other nations and the international community has a direct impact on the welfare of America's people as well as people everywhere.

Globalization creates both challenges and opportunities for nations and the international community. Diplomacy and international peace-keeping are essential in a globalized environment. At the same time, it creates challenges for professions and organizations. Social welfare programs and social work practice require increased attention to and emphasis on the international dimension of the human services. While this changed perspective was apparent in the 20th century, it has become urgently evident in the new millennium. An effective response to the causes and scopes of today's social problems requires both better knowledge of the world scene and more cooperation among nations.

Social work professionals must take action on a number of fronts for social work and social welfare to better respond to the challenges of globalization. More social work involvement in the United Nations and international nongovernmental organizations (NGOs) is needed to help shape global programs aimed at mitigating the negative effects of the global economic system. Social work education programs must strengthen the international dimension of their curricula. Many schools of social work offer courses with international content, but few focus on global issues and practice roles. Cross-national exchange and study abroad programs for social work students are increasing but are still few in number. Many social work educators believe international knowledge is highly specialized and of peripheral use in the practice of most social workers. The challenge of making social work relevant to a global age requires educating educators as well as creating more international learning opportunities for students.

The international institutional framework for social work and social welfare also needs to be strengthened. In *Issues in International Social Work* (1997), Hokenstad and Midgley discuss the importance, but also the limitations, of several international organizations that provide global linkages between professionals and programs. The International Federation of Social Workers (IFSW) and the International Association of Schools of Social Work (IASSW) have active programs that involve social workers from around the world. They provide a social work presence at the United Nations, promoting human rights and supporting refugee, social development, and world health programs. Related international organizations—such as the International Council on Social Welfare (ICSW) and the Inter-University Consortium on International Social Development (IUCISD)—function in the broad area of social welfare and social development, advancing action dealing with global poverty and resulting social problems. All of these organizations do good work, but all are fragile bodies with a small membership and a limited base of financial support. They need to be strengthened financially and organizationally if they are to become effective players on the global playing field.

Many other challenges face social welfare and social work in an age of globalization. Practice roles and organizational structures need to change in order to respond effectively to conditions and problems whose roots extend beyond one nation. New knowledge and innovative service delivery systems are also required. Fortunately, this new age also brings opportunity. Telecommunications technology enhances and encourages the exchange of ideas and information. The sharing of knowledge about programs and practice is accelerated within but also between countries. More information about programs and practices abroad is available, and it can be more readily examined and utilized. There have always been opportunities to learn from other countries, but the new information age provides the means to do this rapidly and thoroughly. As the world grows smaller, exchange of the best practices and programs should become a more normal occurrence.

Models from Other Countries

Lessons from abroad are potentially a key source of both policy ideas and program innovations in social welfare and social work. Recognition and utilization of model programs and best practices from other countries can clearly benefit the United States. This book provides numerous examples of innovations from elsewhere in the world that offer new and different ways of addressing today's social programs. Of course, program innovations originate in many ways. Creative thinking and reflective practice often lead to new or changed practice. Research that evaluates program and practice effectiveness provides a foundation for improvement in providing services. There are many sources of new ideas and different directions in social welfare. But learning from other countries fails to receive the attention it deserves.

Innovative programs from within the United States often receive consideration in the literature and become models for other agencies or even for a nationwide movement such as family preservation. Conferences often disseminate information about the new practice, and, more and more, Web sites highlight the best practices. Information and ideas disseminated in this way sometimes include lessons from abroad, but all too often the models are limited to this country. International journals have a limited readership in the United States and national conferences have difficulty attracting large audiences to international sessions. Hopefully, expanded use of the World Wide Web will help social work professionals learn more about social welfare programs in other parts of the world. The tools for transferring this knowledge are certainly available in this information age.

One needs only to review the history of social welfare and social work to see the importance of learning from other countries. Both the Charity Organization Society and the Settlement House movement, the major roots of voluntary agencies and the social work profession, started in England and were exported to the U.S. A visit to Canon Samuel Barnett's Toynbee Hall in London inspired Jane Addams, arguably the most influential innovator and leader in late 19th- and early 20th-century social welfare, to found Hull House in Chicago. The concept of educated members of a society living and working among poor immigrants was expanded by Addams and others to include community development and social reform as well as neighborhood services. Thus, the adaptation of the British innovation to the cities of the United States had a significant impact on both the shaping of social work and the reform of American society (Axinn & Stern, 2001).

American social welfare policy has also been shaped by models from abroad. During the Great Depression, President Franklin D. Roosevelt sent labor secretary Frances Perkins to Europe to study policies and programs that dealt with poverty, unemployment, and the resulting social unrest. Along with social worker and presidential advisor Harry Hopkins, Perkins proposed the use of social insurance modeled after

European programs to provide old age pensions. This approach to economic security for older people became Title II of the American Social Security Act of 1935. Since that time, social security has been synonymous with old age insurance in the United States. A social innovation developed first in Germany, and then elsewhere in Europe, was adapted into the U.S. social welfare system. It became the cornerstone of the most influential and successful social policy ever enacted in this country (Day, 2000).

Hospice is a good example of a more recent human service innovation from abroad. The hospice movement was started in the 1960s by Dr. Cicely Saunders, a British physician. She established St. Christopher's Hospice near London. It was the first program to use modern pain management techniques to care compassionately for the dying. Hospice has placed emphasis on controlling pain and discomfort when illness no longer responds to cure-oriented treatments. At the same time, a key component of the care is special attention to the social, emotional, and spiritual impact of the disease on both patients and their families. Social workers play a major role in hospice care along with other health care professionals.

Following the British model, the first U.S. hospice was established in 1975 in New Haven, Connecticut. Today, there are more than 3,100 hospices throughout the country. The American adaptation of the model has included hospice care provided in the patient's home as well as residential care. Hospices serve people of all ages who are terminally ill and are an important part of the health care system in this country (Hospice Foundation of America, n.d.).

Lest we consider the developed world as the only source of innovative models, we need only look to Bangladesh, where the first Grameen Bank was set up in 1977, by Muhammed Yunus. The bank was established to provide small loans to groups of landless peasants who had no personal collateral. The loans, which went primarily to groups of women, were used to improve farming capability or to set up small enterprises, such as grocery stores or craft shops. Over the years, the bank has been linked to community development strategies, and, among other projects, has set up a health insurance program on a cost recovery basis. It is now active in 15,000 villages, employs 8,000 workers, and makes loans to half a million people. The bank has a 97.3% on-time repayment record and in recent years has made a profit on its activities (Dauncey, n.d.).

Micro lending to the poor has now spread throughout the world, not only to developing countries but also to the United States. Some banks in this country have adopted Grameen principles, and foundations are providing seed money for nonprofit microenterprise loan companies. Community peer groups make loan decisions in accordance with community development principles. This approach to poverty alleviation and social development has become sufficiently recognized that it is now the subject of political interest and national conferences.

Recent Projects and Future Opportunities

The above examples are innovations from abroad that have had a major impact on social welfare in the United States. Some of the policies and programs examined in this book could have a similar influence in the future. All programs in other nations will not fit the American social welfare system, but many can be adapted to this country's modus operandi as hospice and microlending have in the past. Some overseas imports may have less widespread impact, but still prove useful to some social agencies and community development organizations.

Knowledge about policies and programs in other countries is a first step in making this happen. Recent projects by the social work profession and social work educators in the U.S. have provided information about international innovations in specific program areas. In the early 1990s, the National Association of Social Workers (NASW) carried out a project called "Strengthening Families through International Innovations Transfer." One of its objectives was the international exchange of effective family preservation, reunification, and support initiatives. Descriptions of 33 programs in 17 countries were published in a manual and additional details were provided about exemplary family service models developed in Sweden and Denmark (NASW, 1992). Unfortunately, no information is available about the adoption of these programs in the United States, but it is known that the family circle focus of family and juvenile justice programs in New Zealand has been widely adopted in this country (c.f., chapter 3).

Studies by social work educators have investigated service models in other countries and their potential applicability. For example, Hokenstad and Biederman (1994) examined British initiatives to support family caregivers of older people. They recommended that flexible respite services and caregiver information and support agencies operating in England be utilized in the United States. Additionally, special social work training in caregiver support was recommended based on the British experience. Some of the British innovations were delivered by nonprofit agencies and would fit well within the U.S. service delivery system. Others based on national legislation required new policy in the United States, policy that was enacted in 2000, when a caregiver support system was added to the Older Americans Act in this country.

Some studies have been followed by demonstration projects. Martinez-Brawley and Delevan (1993) report on a demonstration project in rural Pennsylvania that was based on a study of personal social services in the rural counties of England, Scotland, and Wales. The project applied a community-oriented social work strategy that utilized informal networks and was organized around decentralized services. Volunteers also played a very important role in service delivery based on the British experience. While not all aspects of the British approach to service delivery were considered applicable to rural America, some Pennsylvania counties adapted major components. The personal social services demonstration provides a good example of transferring programmatic ideas from another country and applying them locally, while adapting them to a new environment.

This book provides many more examples of program innovations that could be selectively adapted to social welfare programs in the United States. Demonstration projects offer an additional dimension to the determination of appropriate program transfer. Along with program information and exchange visits, such projects can help by providing a direct look at how well overseas programs fit into a different social environment. This is particularly important in the transfer of social programs, because the social support structure helps to determine the success of such programs. Thus, a careful examination of both the innovation and the context in which it is to be implemented is needed.

Innovations from abroad should be adapted to the American human services system rather than simply taken over and used in the original form. Conger (n.d.) points to the importance of social technologies that are needed to match medical technologies that have led to both prevention and cure of disease. Many medical breakthroughs also come from abroad, but the transfer of these innovations is for the most part less problematic than the transfer of social innovations. Solutions to social problems must be adapted into the social, cultural, and political context of each country. Still, the experience of the past demonstrates that this can be done successfully with creative and timely adaptation of these model policies and programs.

The medical example does provide an important lesson for the future. More and more medical breakthroughs are the result of cross-national collaboration. Research is conducted by international teams or at least with ongoing interaction by research teams in different countries. Journals consistently share research findings, including the results of innovations in different countries. Whether related to cancer treatment or bypass surgery, information and evaluation are not only readily available but also effectively used in different nations. This approach to cross-national collaboration is one that should be applied in social welfare research and program innovation.

Great opportunity for learning and sharing internationally is a hallmark of the 21ˢᵗ century. Nations have much to gain from exchanging best practices and policies as they seek to provide social services to vulnerable populations and improve the quality of life for all citizens. Communication technology along with exchange programs and joint research provides a conduit for the sharing of information and ideas. Social work has yet to take full advantage of the increasing opportunity to learn from abroad. This book, with its examples from many countries in different policy and program areas, will hopefully move the profession and U.S. social welfare in that direction.

Scope and Content of the Book

Lessons from Abroad discusses examples of current international policies and programs that can serve as models for the United States and its social welfare system. Each chapter examines a different content area. Some chapters address programs in specific fields, such as mental health, child welfare, and aging, while others look more broadly at poverty alleviation, social security, and social development. Finally, there is a chapter on international treaties and conventions that impact social welfare policies and programs. All chapters provide an in-depth look at innovative policies and programs and then draw implications for the United States.

The topics selected for examination in this book certainly do not exhaust the subject areas that provide lessons from abroad in the field of social welfare. Chapters on programs addressing domestic violence and substance abuse could have been included. Disaster relief services and refugee support offered by different countries are also pertinent areas of inquiry. These subjects along with environmental protection, housing programs, and health care could easily provide the content for another book. The chapters of this book reflect the editors' choice of some key areas of international interest coupled with space limitations rather than all-inclusive coverage of social welfare models from abroad.

In Chapter 2, Guseilo, Curl, and Hokenstad examine European policy and program innovations designed to meet the challenge of aging populations and to improve the lives of older people. These include workforce policies and practices that encourage employers to recruit and retrain older workers, pension reforms that emphasize flexibility with a focus on gradual retirement, and financing long-term care through a universal social insurance program. Finally, the authors offer the example of a British suicide-prevention program entitled "Saving Lives: Our Healthier Nation" as a model for lowering older adult suicide rates in the United States. Since European nations are demographically older than the United States, the best practices discussed in this chapter could help our nation meet the challenges faced as the baby boomer generation reaches retirement age.

Katherine van Wormer explores international innovations in child welfare in Chapter 3. First, she reviews recent innovations that the United States has already borrowed from elsewhere in the world. These include family group conferencing from New Zealand and shared family care from Denmark. Her discussion takes a look at how states and agencies have adapted these and other models to the American experience. She also evaluates innovative programs that originated in the U.S. such as family preservation services. Van Wormer emphasizes the difficulty of implementing program innovations without a strong social support system. The lack of a children's allowance and a universal health care system in the United States make service innovations more difficult to adopt here.

Social security privatization through the use of individual retirement accounts is currently a hotly debated policy issue in the United States. In Chapter 4, James Midgley examines the use of different forms of individual retirement accounts in three different countries: Chile, which uses commercially managed retirement accounts; Singapore, which uses provident funds invested and managed by the government; and Great Britain, which has a combination pension program, including a stakeholder (individual retirement) program. Midgley points to both strengths and weaknesses of the various systems and to a particular problem for low-income people in accumulating enough savings to meet retirement income needs. He concludes that retirement accounts should not be created at the expense of the basic social security system.

Neil Gilbert scrutinizes work-oriented income support programs in Chapter 5. He examines a number of active work-oriented welfare measures in Europe and compares them with the U.S. experience with the Temporary Assistance for Needy Families (TANF) program. He points out that although lessons must be based on solid empirical evidence, which is still lacking in many areas, there are some conclusions that can be drawn from the available choices. Aggregate empirical evidence shows that the U.S. approach is less effective than other advanced industrial countries, if the objective is not simply to get people off welfare roles but also to provide income security and prevent poverty. Thus, the United States could benefit by knowledge of the experiences in France, the Netherlands, Scandinavia, and other European countries.

Mental health lessons from abroad are the focus of Chapter 6. Janice Wetzel begins this chapter by emphasizing that to be effective, mental health programs must give attention to social and economic conditions in addition to considering biological and psychological indicators. There is a need to focus on at-risk populations as well as individuals suffering from mental illness. She then discusses community-based programs around the world that address the multiple dimensions of public health. These include programs for battered women and battering men in Australia, Canada, and Israel. Wetzel also considers social and economic development programs for poor women. Finally, she turns her attention to mental disabilities and gives examples of European "social firms" that provide employment for the mentally disabled.

Lessons from the global south are the subject of Chapter 7. James Midgley and Michelle Livermore identify social development projects and programs that link social welfare to economic development in order to meet the needs of poor communities. They show how this developmental approach has been applied in the establishment of day care centers in India, community improvement projects in West Africa, and microenterprises in the Philippines. Then they discuss how the same principles and process of social development could be applied in the United States. A persuasive case is made for the relevance of social development to the problem of poverty in this country.

United Nations treaties and conventions on human rights are concerned not only with civil and political rights, but also with economic, social, and cultural rights. In the book's final chapter, Elizabeth Lightfoot provides a thorough examination of different types of international agreements and then discusses their relevance for the social welfare of people around the world. She points specifically to the Convention on the Rights of the Child and the Convention on the Elimination of All Forms of Discrimination against Women as important international agreements that the United States has yet to ratify, and considers the reasons why this country has failed to act. Then she considers how policy goals and ideas, such as the framing of children's issues in terms of rights, can still be borrowed from these treaties. Even though ratification is preferable, the language of these treaties can influence policies and practices in the U.S., as well as other countries.

References

Axinn, J., & Stern, M. (2001). *Social welfare: A history of the American response to need* (5th ed). Boston: Allyn & Bacon.

Conger, S. (n.d.). The history of social inventions. Retrieved from http://www.globalideasbank.org/BOV/BV-2.HTML on July 1, 2002.

Dauncey, G. (n.d.). Grameen banks for the poorest of the poor. Retrieved from http://www.globalideasbank.org/BOV/BV-521.html July 1, 2002.

Day, P. (2000). *A new history of social welfare* (3rd ed.). Needham Heights, MA: Allyn & Bacon.

Friedman, T.L. (2000). *The lexus and the olive tree*. New York: Anchor Books.

Hokenstad, M.C., & Biederman, C.A. (1994). *Model of caregiver support: British initiatives*. Cleveland: Case Western Reserve University, Mandel School of Applied Social Sciences.

Hokenstad, M.C., & Midgley, J. (1997). *Issues in international social work: Global challenges for a new century*. Washington, DC: NASW Press.

Hospice Foundation of America (n.d.). What is hospice? Retrieved from http://www.hospicefoundation.org on July 5, 2002.

Martinez-Brawley, E., & Delevan, S. (1993). *Transferring technology in the personal social services*. Washington, DC: NASW Press.

National Association of Social Workers (1992). *Strengthening families through international innovations transfer: A directory of programs, consultants, and resource materials*. Washington, DC: NASW.

CHAPTER TWO

Policies and Programs in Aging: International Initiatives

James A. Guseilo, Angela L. Curl, AND M. C. Hokenstad

The world's population is expanding exponentially, and the over-60 population growth is accelerating at a faster rate than the overall population. By 2025, the United Nations (UN) estimates the world's population will be 8.2 billion, which is double that of 1975 (UN, 2000). During that same time frame, the population of persons 60 years and older will have increased to about 15 percent of the projected total population (UN, 2002a). In 1975, persons 60 years and older were equally distributed between developed and developing countries. The UN estimates that by 2025, 72 percent of that population segment will be living in today's developing countries (UN, 2000).

At the dawn of the 21st century the over-65 population of the United States is approaching 13 percent of the total population, and is projected to rise to over 20 percent by 2030 (Administration on Aging, 2000). This over-60 age distribution is partially due to the gradual aging of 77 million post-World War II "baby boomers." The number of Americans 65 and older increased by 10.5 percent from 1990 to 1999, and will continue to increase, according to the U.S. Census Bureau (2000a). The Bureau projects that by the middle of the 21st century, there will be as many people age 85 and older in the United States as there will be people age 65 to 69.

Aging-related issues will increase in magnitude with the sheer numbers of the world's expanding population. As we consider the seriousness of this challenge for developed countries, one must also recognize the magnitude of this problem for developing countries such as China, where 13 percent of more than one billion citizens will be over the age of 60 by 2025 (George, 1997). During the first half of the 21st century, population aging will become a major issue in the developing world. Developed countries have been able to age gradually, but they still face the challenges of affordable health care and sustainability of pension programs. Developing countries face the challenge of simultaneous economic development and population aging (UN, 2000).

Twenty percent or more of the population of many nations in the European Union (EU) are over age 60 (UN, 2002b). Thus, these countries are already grappling with issues the United States is likely to face. Knowledge developed today in Europe through experiences with these demographically older populations can potentially be transferred across national and geographic boundaries to contribute answers to challenges that are ahead for the United States.

This chapter examines European policy and program innovations relating to older adults that can provide insight into challenges that the U.S. will face in the future. In the United States, people are considered "older adults" when they reach the age of 65. This age marker is a socially constructed category. The age of 65 for old-age insurance eligibility was assigned to the United States Social Security legislation based on an actuarial study and the prevailing state and private pension plans (Social Security Administration [SSA], "Age 65 retirement," n.d.). The United Nations uses the age of 60 for its statistical purposes.

Today's developing economies are converting from industrial societies to societies that specialize in information and knowledge production. Accompanying the birth of this economic revolution are declining birth rates and increased longevity. Aging-related topics discussed in this chapter include the aging workforce, pension support, long-term care and caregiver support, and elder suicide. These are but a few of the challenges in an aging society but they provide good examples of actions taken by other nations that could lead to innovative aging policies and programs in the United States.

Aging Workforce and Labor Market Policy

In 1998, the AARP conducted a poll of U.S. baby boomers' retirement plans. It found that 80 percent of the boomers, then ages 37 to

54, planned to work at least part-time past age 65 (AARP, 1998). In 1998, older Americans comprised only 2.8 percent of the workforce (National Council on the Aging, 2000). However, several factors will contribute to the percent of older workers in the future labor market. These include societal forces such as skilled labor shortages and fewer young people entering the labor market. They also include individual motivation related to financial necessity and improved health at older ages. As nations change from industrial to information-based economies, the rationale for retirement will also change.

In the past, developed societies emphasized getting older workers out of the labor market. Forced retirement age limits and early retirement incentive programs were used to lower business costs and unemployment rates. The rationale for mandatory retirement policies in Europe and the United States was to provide more job opportunities for young people. However, it was also motivated by ageism, the systematic stereotyping of and discrimination against people because of their age (Loretto & Duncan, 2000). The United States now has age discrimination legislation protecting older workers in the labor market, and the U.S. Equal Employment Opportunity Commission (EEOC) reports that one in five EEOC charges are related to age discrimination (U.S. EEOC, 2000). On the other hand, most European nations still have mandatory retirement ages, but Europe is using other policies and programs to improve employment opportunities for older workers.

Workforce aging policy has been a dedicated focus of the European Union since 1994. The Essen Summit directly addressed improving employment opportunities for older workers, while the Cardiff and Vienna Councils emphasized inclusion of older workers in the development of a skilled and adaptable workforce (Naegele, 1999). A 1994 European Union study concluded that initiatives to combat age barriers were best focused on "good practices" of retention, reintegration and retraining of older workers. This strategy has been adopted by EU countries.

Implementing "good practice" has translated differently in member countries' policy approaches. In the United Kingdom the focus is on job recruitment and flexible work practices. German and Dutch policy is primarily aimed at training the workforce. In each of the above cases government policy is aimed at replacing early retirement incentives with job creation and retention incentives (European Foundation for the Improvement of Living and Working Conditions, 1997).

Governments are encouraging commercial companies to combat age barriers with training programs intended to retain a balanced intergenerational mix in the workplace.

In the next decade, the European workforce will continue its demographic shift. Declining birth rates have produced a shrinking workforce that is living longer and needing to work longer. Knowledge gained over a work life and transferred to the youthful workforce is a valuable asset to companies and society. National and regional governments are now taking a number of steps, including the direct financing of employment policy initiatives. These include encouraging employers to recruit and retrain older workers to be efficient and productive for competition in an age neutral global economy (Naegele, 1999).

The EU has assumed the role of disseminating 'good practice' examples throughout the Union with the publication of *Combating Age Barriers in Employment: A European Portfolio of Good Practice* (Walker & Taylor, 1998). The report contains 155 examples of Swedish, UK, Italian, Dutch, German, French, Greek, Belgian, and Finnish private enterprise "good practice" under the dimensions of job recruitment; training, development and promotion; flexible working practices; ergonomics/job design and changing attitudes within organizations. After reviewing the "good practices," Walker (1998) concludes that all members of the European labor market have a role to play in creating the conditions for "good practice." The European social partners are taking the first steps that others will follow: Employers are developing age awareness, aging workers are taking advantage of training opportunities, and trade unions are including training measures to update older workers' skills. Also, national employer organizations are disseminating examples of good practice, and governments are financing, regulating, and opposing age barriers. These good practice examples provide ideas and innovations for countries both within and outside of the European Union.

Pension Policy

Social Security policy moved to the forefront of aging issue discussions during the last decades of the 20th century. Demographic change and its economic impact are leading to revolutionary changes in pension policy. The most pressing issue in pension policy is the solvency of pay-as-you-go (PAYG) social security established in the late 19th and 20th centuries. Traditional pension schemes rely on ongoing contributions of the current workforce to fund pensions for those who have retired, and those currently contributing will rely on contributions by future generations to pay for their public pensions. In the first half of the 21st century it is projected that there will be fewer and fewer workers available to support an exponentially growing number of retirees, creating funding problems for current pension policies.

In the United States, retirement of the baby boom generation will begin to heavily draw upon pension systems in the second decade of the 21st century. In 1990, there were five workers contributing to the pension system for every one retiree withdrawing from the system; that ratio will fall to three workers for every one retiree by 2020 (Reday-Mulvey, 2000). Also, older people are living longer in their post-retirement years. The increasing post-60 life expectancy trend was coupled with a trend towards earlier retirements in the latter half of the 20th century. The combination of these factors will increase the number of years that any one person is likely to draw a public pension. This increase of pension-drawing time, added to the overall growth in the number of pensioners, has produced what many call the "pension crises" (Hokenstad & Johansson, 2001).

Changing population patterns have implications for both financing pensions and filling the labor force. While the latter is not yet a major policy issue in the United States, because of substantial rates of immigration, it is of growing concern for the aging societies of Europe. The previously discussed European programs and policies, which are being implemented by governments, attempt to address issues related to their aging workforce. As that workforce enters retirement, additional issues of financial security and affordable health care require attention. As the requirement for an age-neutral intergenerational workforce is combined with the knowledge production economy, retirement policies will need to address the convergence of labor, technology and capital markets (MacKellar, Ermolieva, & Reisen, 1999).

The theme for pensions today in Europe emphasizes flexibility with a focus on gradual retirement. Pension p licy reforms recently enacted in the EU include provisions for a rise in retirement age eligibility, gradual retirement, and partial pensions. In addition, early retirement incentive programs enacted twenty years ago are being phased out as costly and counterproductive to maintaining a trained and skilled workforce. The intent is to keep trained, productive, contributing employees on the job, thereby adding to the economic base and reducing the burden on social pension expenditure. In order to control escalating wage costs and to motivate productivity, seniority-based compensation plans are being replaced by wages based on performance. These changes have required cooperation and flexibility between employers and employees throughout the world.

Pension policy is being used by many countries as a motivator to keep older people in the workforce longer. The most obvious way to do this is to increase the age at which a full pension can be received. In the United States, the age for receiving full benefits is being increased from 65 years to 67 years (SSA, 1984). This change is being instituted over an extended period of time, but there is already political debate over the further extension of the full benefit age to 70. As one of many proposals put forward to guarantee the long-term fiscal solvency of the social security system, such pension age proposals, if enacted, will extend the work life of many workers—particularly those who cannot afford to retire without a full pension.

Another type of pension reform has just been enacted in the United States. Legislation passed in 2000 eliminated the retirement earnings test for workers at the normal age of full retirement and older (SSA, n.d.). This means that workers are now entitled to full social security benefits at the age of full retirement regardless of their current employment status and the amount of income that they earn from their jobs. There is no longer a financial penalty for older workers continuing in the labor market, either full or part time. This policy uncouples retirement from pension policy by no longer limiting pension payments to retired workers.

It is too early to determine the impact of this policy on retirement patterns in the United States. Empirical evidence will be available in a few years. Yet it is safe to assume that the working lives of many Americans will be extended now that there is no longer a financial incentive to retire at the normal age of full retirement. Many people will be encouraged to work longer, as the policy will reinforce flexible retirement patterns and promote positive attitudes toward longer working lives. Thus, this pension reform uses the "carrot rather than the stick" approach to keep people working longer (Hokenstad & Johansson, 2001).

European pension reform also reflects changing demographics and patterns of work. Sweden's new pension policy, which was fully implemented in 2001, encourages later retirement by basing the amount of the pension on the remaining life expectancy of the pensioner (Sundén, 2000). At the same time, it promotes flexibility in retirement by providing partial pensions for partial retirement any time after age 61. This combination of policy provisions should impact work as well as retirement patterns in Sweden.

Sweden's pension policy is of particular interest for two reasons. First, Sweden is one of the demographically oldest societies in the world. In fact, it had the oldest population until Italy surpassed it in 2000 (U.S. Census Bureau, 2001). Approximately 17 percent of all Swedes are now 65 years of age or older (U.S. Census Bureau, 2000b). Low fertility rates and increasing longevity will mean the continued aging of the Swedish population. It is useful to look at a country that is approximately 20 years ahead of the United States in the aging trajectory.

Also, social and political commitments make old age security and elder care a central feature of an expansive social protection system in Sweden. Its income support and social service programs provide cradle-to-grave security for the Swedish people. Public policy provides the funding and the framework for the provision of programs that have substantially eliminated poverty and reduced the incidence of associated health and human problems. The Swedish pension program is a cornerstone of a health and welfare system that also includes national health insurance; housing allowances; and comprehensive home, community, and long-term care services for older citizens.

The increasing number of old age pensioners in proportion to the working population has created a challenge to the elder care commitment in Sweden. The increased cost of pension payments is the major reason for pension reform. At the same time, it is considered important to redress inequities in the system. The new pension plan has restructured benefits based on lifetime earnings and linked the pension amount to economic growth.

Another significant change provides pension credits for time devoted to caring for children and for time in postsecondary education. This provision gives more than "lip service" to the importance of parenting. Pension entitlement is received for stay-at-home childcare during the first four years of the child's life. While childcare at home can be credited to the pension account of either parent, it is likely to go most often to the mother's account. This will promote gender equity in pension payments—a progressive step in pension reform. In addition, pension entitlement credits for time spent in higher education degree programs help promote a well-educated workforce.

All of these areas of pension reform are important, but the inclusion of retirement age flexibility in the reform is particularly significant. Under the new system, pensions are payable in Sweden when a person reaches the age of 61 (International Reform Monitor, n.d.). There is no fixed retirement age, and there is nothing to prevent a person from working and receiving a pension at the same time. However, by continuing to work, a worker will increase her or his annual pension in two ways: Pension credits based on salary will increase pension assets, and pension credits not used will accumulate for the future. These are incentives for later retirement. The later a person decides to retire, the greater the pension.

In addition to the flexible pension age, the Swedish reform provides flexibility in the amount of pension taken. The pension can be drawn in full or in fractions of one-quarter, one-half or three-quarters of full pension any time from age 61 to age 70 (Schremmer, 1999). At the latter age, a full pension must be drawn. These options of partial pensions offer flexibility in retirement planning and quite likely will have an impact on retirement patterns (Hokenstad & Johansson, 2001).

The Swedish reform is a good example of the considerable amount of policy action taking place in the countries of the European Union. Many member states are enacting changes in pension policy to stem the flow of older workers out of the labor market. These include encouraging part-time work rather than retirement. Austria, Belgium, Denmark, Finland, France, Germany, Italy, and the Netherlands have all taken some action, resulting in the growth of part-time employment among both female and male older workers.

Other European countries also have been active in reforming their pension systems. In Germany, the "Pension Reform 2000" bill was introduced on September 22, 2000, focusing on individual funded pension accounts based on a defined contribution scheme and compulsory annuitization (Nocker, 2000). The new system in private pension provision will be phased in. The objective is to increase individual contribution rates from half a percent of eligible salary for pensions in

2001 to 4 percent in 2004 through a system of individual tax breaks and a capped state contribution. The bill proposes compulsory annuitization of the contributed funds through unit trusts, mutual funds or other investment funds regulated by the European investment directives.

In the Netherlands, a government-regulated private system of fully-funded supplementary pensions is required as an addition to the social security system to compensate for shortfalls in government fiscal capacity. In France, a proposal has been raised to establish a central reserve fund in anticipation of the looming demographic crisis. This should offset an assumed 2 percent economic growth rate that cannot sustain the anticipated strain on the PAYG social security system in the decades ahead (Clark, 2001). These pension reforms have been coupled with flexible retirement plans and partial pension programs in order to keep workers in the labor force longer and maintain the fiscal solvency of the system.

Pension policy will continue to be modified to meet the challenge of demographic aging. European pension reforms need careful attention as the United States debates policy options for social security.

Long-term Care

On January 1, 1995, the Federal Republic of Germany closed a twenty-year debate over long-term care insurance when "Pflegeversicherung" was enacted, establishing a non-means-tested entitlement program separate from the national healthcare program, with a capped budget and fixed benefit. As of that day, eighty-one million people in Germany who were previously covered by statutory health insurance were automatically also covered with long-term care insurance. The German Federal Ministry of Labour and Social Affairs (Federal Ministry) defines long-term care assistance and describes the eligibility criteria (2001):

> According to the law, you are eligible if you require frequent or substantial help with normal day-to-day activities on a long-term basis (that is, for an estimated six months or longer). Four different areas—personal hygiene, eating, mobility and housekeeping— are taken into account when determining whether you need assistance (2001, p. 86).

Taking into account the annexation of the Democratic Republic of Germany (East Germany), Germany has had a relatively stable population in total numbers. In 1975, the total population of Germany was 78.7 million, in 1997, it was 82.1 million, and for 2015 the projected population is 81.6 million (UN, 1999). During the last 25 years there has been a major demographic trend toward population aging. In 1997, 15.7 percent of German citizens were 60 years or older. The projection for 2015 is that 20.3 percent of the population will fall into the 60-plus category. That is an increase of almost four million citizens, or a growth rate of 30 percent over eighteen years. Embedded within the growth statistic is an expanding life expectancy of German citizens. In 1997 the life expectancy of females was 80.2 years, and 73.9 years for males. While the population of Germany is static, it is aging. An older population means increased need for long-term care.

Historically, there was a legal distinction between the universal social insurance health care program and long-term care in Germany (Cuellar & Wiener, 1999). Long-term care costs were shared between the state (Laender) and local governments and administered through a means-tested welfare program restricted to those who were poor or who had "spent down" to poverty. Aging demographics, the integration of East Germany, and a rapidly rising institutional long-term care fiscal burden caused the Laender to turn to the federal government of Germany for relief.

The Federal government negotiated and set forth a number of policy goals. Policymakers needed to develop an easily understood, non-means-tested, long-term care program that provided fiscal relief to the Laender and established eligibility criteria for services based on available funds. They were also charged with expanding home-based services, supporting informal caregivers, and developing competitive provider markets.

Three alternative delivery methods were proposed to accomplish the policy goals. The first proposal was a federal program similar to the universal healthcare system. The program, funded through general revenue was rejected as being cost prohibitive. Second, a mandatory private insurance program was considered, but rejected because it did not address the socially responsible ethic valued by Germans. Finally, a hybrid social insurance program with capped benefits, in which all participants receive like benefits, seemed to fit both fiscal reality and the cultural ethic of social responsibility (Cuellar & Wiener, 1999).

The line between public and private institutions and between taxes and premiums is not as distinct in Germany as it is in the United States. The new universal social insurance funded program was implemented in 1995. It provides coverage for all citizens regardless of their financial status or needs. The Germans view their program as social insurance with defined benefits. The universal program provides custodial care for personal hygiene, eating, mobility, and housekeeping (Federal Ministry, 2001). Each of these categories of care is provided based on a three-tier consideration for daily levels of care required:

- Care Level I Considerable—help needed at least once a day
- Care Level II Severe—help needed at least three times a day
- Care Level III Extreme—help needed 24 hours a day

Each of the three levels of care is funded whether the individual is cared for in an institution or at home (Federal Ministry, 2001). While the care level need criteria remain constant, institutional and home care reimbursement rates differ. Services delivered through the home-care option are reimbursed at half the rate of institutional care. The home-care choice offers the patient the option to receive care services from the marketplace or from family members while remaining at home (Cuellar & Wiener, 1999). A key goal of the German long-term care policy initiative was to shift the locus of care from institutions to the home. Prior to this reform, the preponderance of care was delivered in institutions. The Laender bore the brunt of the fiscal cost, and the people bore the price of being isolated from their families.

The program, beginning with the home-care portion, was phased in over a period of months. To further emphasize the benefits of home-care, several additional features were built into the home-care option beyond those offered by the standard services included in the institutional portion of the funded program. These included nursing aids, such as special beds needed for home-based long-term care, and some funds for home modifications (Federal Ministry, 2001).

Informal caregivers were targeted for special consideration. The Federal Ministry defined informal caregivers as anyone providing unpaid home nursing care for at least 14 hours a week. The long-term care insurance fund contributes statutory pension payments for those caregivers not employed or working less than 30 hours per week (Federal Ministry, 2001). In addition, caregivers are offered free nursing care courses and up to four weeks a year of respite stand-in services, paid through the insurance fund.

The German long-term care social insurance program is funded through incremental payroll contributions. Because the program delivers fixed entitlement benefits to all citizens, the long-term care assessment for each worker is a flat 1.7 percent of earned wages, up to a maximum cap fixed by legislation. The 1.7 percent assessment rate is added to the 32.6 percent payroll assessment already paid for health and pension benefits. The 1.7 percent rate is set by law and will not automatically be increased to cover expenditures beyond the capped spending budget. Employees and employers share the 1.7 percent payroll assessment equally. In order to ameliorate the additional employer costs of this program, a paid federal holiday was eliminated (Scheiwe, 1997).

Current data indicates that Pflegeversicherung has been successful in reducing overall care cost by shifting long-term delivery from institutional services to a lower-cost cash benefit option paid directly to home caregivers. According to the Federal Ministry, as of 1997, almost three-quarters of beneficiaries were in non-institutional settings, waiting lists to enter institutions had disappeared, and the number of registered caregivers tripled in two years. Fifty-eight percent of long-term care expenditures were for cash benefits, home-care and pension contributions for caregivers, and the insurance program ran a surplus.

Prior to the enactment of Pflegeversicherung, Germany had a long-term care system similar to that of the means-tested Medicaid program of the United States. Both Germany and the United States face an increase in elder age distribution exceeding 20 percent of their total population and similar female/male life expectancy rates. While the age-distribution of Germany is 30 years ahead of that of the United States, the pressures on long-term care services are the same. Germany's long-term care policy used the terminology "spend down to poverty" to describe their pre-1995 means-tested program. The same phraseology is used today to characterize the means-tested Medicaid program in the United States. The Germans have replaced a bankrupt system with home-care incentives now recognize caregivers and place emphasis on independent living for senior citizens at a fixed cost of 1.7 percent of capped salary (Federal Ministry, 2001).

Elder Suicide

Suicide is a multidimensional event, and to understand the complexity of elder suicide risk there needs to be an exploration of psychological as well as sociological theory. Emile Durkheim (1858–1917) postulated the preeminent sociological theory on suicide. According to Durkheim, the term "[s]uicide is applied to all cases of death resulting directly or indirectly from a positive or negative act of the victim himself, which he knows will produce this result." (1951, p. 2)

Durkheim proposed three categories of risk for suicide: egoistic, altruistic and anomic. People who feel alienated from others and have too little social integration are more likely to commit "egoistic" suicides. In contrast, people who commit "altruistic" suicides feel so much a part of the group that they lose sight of their individuality and sacrifice themselves for what they believe to be the good of the group. Durkheim's third category, "anomic" suicides, refers to suicides triggered by a sudden change in a person's relationship to society. Durkheim categorized anomic suicide as an imbalance of means and needs, where means were unable to fulfill needs (Davison & Neale, 1998). The weakness of this theory is its inability to account for the differences among individual reactions to the same demands and conditions in a society, as well as its poor applicability to non-European nations (Lester & Abe, 1998).

Psychological theories also explain suicide, predict risk factors, and suggest prevention strategies. According to Leenaars (1999), developmental age plays a significant factor in why people kill themselves. Life tasks of older adults can become overwhelming stressors with the accumulation of loss including the ongoing deficit in personality functioning. In developed societies the depressed, widowed, divorced, and recently bereaved are at higher risk of suicide. Life events commonly associated with elderly suicide are "the death of a loved one; physical illness, uncontrollable pain; fear of dying a prolonged death, social isolation and loneliness; and major changes in social roles" (McIntosh, n.d., p. 1).

Throughout the world, the latter part of life is a time of accumulating loss: job, social status, health and independence. In the Western world, 5 percent of the elderly manifest these losses in stress, depression and hopelessness at a time when individuals are most susceptible to suicidal thoughts. According to 1998 National Center for Health Statistics data, on average one person 65 and older years of age killed him- or herself every one-and-a-half hours in the United States in that year (McIntosh, 2000). In 1998, those 65 and older made up 12.7 percent of the total U.S. population, but committed 19 percent of the suicides. Depression, the most frequent psychiatric disorder in the elderly (Stoppe, Sandholzer, Huppertz, Duwe, & Staedt, 1999), afflicts up to 5 percent of people aged 65 and older (McIntosh, n.d.).

Recent studies in the U.S. have revealed under-identification and under-treatment of depression among older suicide victims. Physicians tend not to recognize depression and suicide ideation in the elderly. According to one study, nearly 40 percent of older people had seen their primary care doctors during the week prior to committing suicide (Conwell, 1994). Physician education is necessary for doctors to learn to recognize and treat depression as well as how to talk to the elderly about the complex issue of suicide. National attention should be given to improving identification and intervention programs.

Such action is being taken in some other countries. For example, in 1999, the British government introduced a white paper, *Saving Lives: Our Healthier Nation,* which proposed a program to reduce the suicide rate by one-sixth of its 1996 rate by 2010 (Hoxey & Shah, 2000). England and Wales expect to achieve their goal of improved detection of those elderly who are at risk for suicide. Strategies for reducing suicide rates among the elderly include senior peer counseling, improved mental health services through suicide prevention centers and improved suicide risk awareness among those who have frequent contact with seniors. Already, legislation has been enacted in the United Kingdom encouraging general practitioners to offer both annual physical and mental examinations to those over 75 years old. The social welfare structure of England and Wales is attempting to help older workers function in an increasingly competitive workforce. These policy innovations suggest strategies for the United States to pursue in the goal to reduce elder suicide in this nation.

Conclusion

In 2004, many European nations have significantly greater percentages of their population over the age of 60 than the United States. As life expectancies increase and birth rates decrease, the global aging trend will continue, accompanied by numerous fiscal and social policy issues. Knowledge and expertise developed through new policies and programs in European nations can be utilized by other nations, including the United States. Some areas of European policy innovations presented in this chapter relate to retirement, pensions, long-term care, and elder suicide prevention. These innovations promote "best practice" policies that are socially and fiscally responsible, offer flexibility to meet individual needs, and recognize the value of older adults.

The *Madrid International Plan of Action on Ageing*, adopted by the United Nations in April of 2002, points out that program innovation, mobilization of financial resources, and development of human resources are all needed as governments and civil societies strive to meet the challenges of demographic aging (UN, 2002a). Nations are called upon to exchange experiences and best practices as they seek to implement the plan's action priorities in the areas of older persons and development, advancing health and well-being into old age, and ensuring enabling and supportive environments for older people. Along with research and information dissemination, innovations from abroad such as those discussed in this chapter are recognized as one major approach to meeting the challenge of population aging and thereby improving the lives of older people.

References

AARP. (1998). *Boomers look toward retirement*. Washington, DC: Research Group, AARP.

Administration on Aging. (2000). *A profile of older Americans: 2000*. Washington, DC: U.S. Department of Health and Human Services. Retrieved August 2, 2001, from http://www.aoa.gov/aoa/stats/profile/profile2000-bw.pdf

Clark, G. L. (2001). *European pensions and global finance: Continuity or convergence?* Oxford, UK: University of Oxford.

Conwell, Y. (1994). Suicide in elderly patients. In L. S. Schneider, C. F. Reynolds III, B. D. Lebowitz, & A. J. Friedhoff (Eds.), *Diagnosis and treatment of depression in late life* (pp. 397–418). Washington, DC: American Psychiatric Press.

Cuellar, A. E., & Wiener, J. M. (1999). Structuring a universal long-term-care program: The experience in Germany. *Generations, 13*(2), 45–50.

Davison, G. C., & Neale, J. M. (1998). *Abnormal psychology*. New York: Wiley.

Durkheim, E. (1951). *Suicide: A study in sociology*. (J. Spaulding & G. Simpson, Trans.). Glencoe, IL: Free Press. (Original work published 1897)

European Foundation for the Improvement of Living and Working Conditions. (1997). *Combating age barriers in employment: Research summary*. Luxembourg, Germany: Office for Official Publications of the European Communities.

Federal Ministry of Labour and Social Affairs. (2001). *Social security at a glance.* Retrieved May 13, 2002, from http://www.bma.bund.de/download/broschueren/A998.pdf

George, J. (1997). Global graying. In M. C. Hokenstad & J. Midgley (Eds.), *Issues in international social work: Global challenges for a new century* (pp. 57–73). Washington, DC: NASW Press.

Hokenstad, M. C., & Johansson, L. (2001). Retirement patterns and pension policy: An international perspective. In F. L. Ahearn (Ed.), *Issues in global aging* (pp. 25–32). New York: Haworth Press.

Hoxey, K., & Shah, A. (2000). Recent trends in elderly suicide rates in England and Wales. *International Journal of Geriatric Psychiatry, 15,* 274–279.

International Reform Monitor. (n.d.). Pension provision (Sweden). Retrieved May 25, 2002, from http://www.reformmonitor.org/httpd-cache/doc_stq_pp-163.html

Leenaars, A. A. (1999). Suicide across the adult life span: Replications and failures. *Archives of Suicide Research, 5,* 261–274.

Lester, D., & Abe, K. (1998). The suicide rate by each method in Japan: A test of Durkheim's theory of suicide. *Archives of Suicide Research, 4,* 281–285.

Loretto, W., & Duncan, C. (2000). Ageism and employment: Controversies, ambiguities and younger people's perceptions. *Ageing and Society, 20,* 279–302.

MacKellar, L., Ermolieva, T., & Reisen, H. (1999). *Globalization, social security, and intergenerational transfers.* Laxenburg, Austria: International Institute for Applied Systems Analysis.

McIntosh, J. L. (n.d.). *The suicide of older men and women: How you can help prevent tragedy.* Retrieved November 22, 2000, from http://www.suicidology.org/older_men_and_women.htm

McIntosh, J. L. (2000). *U.S.A. suicide: 1998 official final data.* American Association of Suicidology. Retrieved November 22, 2000, from http://www.iusb.edu/~jmcintos/USA98Summary.htm

Naegele, G. (1999). *Active strategies for an ageing workforce: Conference report.* Luxembourg, Germany: European Foundation for the Improvement of Living and Working Conditions, Office for Official Publications of the European Communities.

National Council on the Aging. (2000). *Facts about older Americans.* Retrieved May 13, 2002, from http://www.ncoa.org/press/facts.html

Nocker, R. (2000). *The recent proposals for individual funded pensions in Germany—repeating the UK experience?* London: Centre for Pensions and Social Insurance, Birkbeck College, University of London.

Reday-Mulvey, G. (2000). Gradual retirement in Europe. *Journal of Aging & Social Policy II* (2/3), 49–69.

Scheiwe, K. (1997). *New demands for social protection—changing family structures, women's roles and institutional responses: The case of the German Long-Term Care Insurance.* Retrieved January 21, 2002, from http://www.mzes.uni-mannheim.de/publications/wp/wp1-19.pdf

Schremmer, J. (1999). *Public policy and the retirement decision: Early, partial and deferred retirement in selected countries.* Geneva, Switzerland: International Social Security Association Research Programme.

Social Security Administration. (n.d.). You can work and get Social Security at the same time. Retrieved May 25, 2002, from http://www.ssa.gov/retire2/whileworking.htm

Social Security Administration. (2000, April 7). *The President signs the "Senior Citizens' Freedom to Work Act of 2000."* Retrieved May 25, 2002, from www.ssa.gov/legislation/legis_bulletin_040700.html

Social Security Administration. (n.d.). *Age 65 retirement.* Retrieved May 25, 2002, from www.ssa.gov/history.age65.html

Social Security Administration. (1984). *Summary of P.L. 98-21, (H.R. 1900). Social Security amendments of 1983—signed on April 20, 1983.* Retrieved May 25, 2002, from http://www.ssa.gov/history/1983amend.html

Stoppe, G., Sandholzer, H., Huppertz, C., Duwe, H., & Staedt, J. (1999). Family physicians and the risk of suicide in the depressed elderly. *Journal of Affective Disorders, 54,* 193–198.

Sundén, A. (2000, March). *How will Sweden's new pension system work? Executive summary.* (Issue Brief No. 3). Boston, MA: Center for Retirement Research. Retrieved May 25, 2002, from http://www.bc.edu/bc_org/avp/csom/executive/crr/issues/ib_3.pdf

United Nations Development Program. (1999). *Human development reports 1990 to 1999.* New York: Oxford University Press.

United Nations. (2000). *International plan of action on ageing.* Retrieved August 8, 2001, from http://www.un.org/esa/socdev/ageing/ageipaa.htm

United Nations. (2002a). *Madrid international plan of action on ageing 2002.* Retrieved May 13, 2002, from http://www.un.org/ageing/coverage/action.pdf

United Nations. (2002b). Indicators on youth and elderly populations. Retrieved July 9, 2002, http://unstats.un.org/unsd/demographic/social/youth.htm

United States Census Bureau. (2000a). *Population estimates for countries by age groups, July 1, 1990 to July 1, 1999.* Retrieved January 17, 2001, from http://www.census.gov/population/estimates/county/ca/caus.txt

United States Census Bureau. (2000b). *The world's 25 oldest countries: 2000*. Retrieved May 25, 2002, from http://www.census.gov/Press-Release/www/2001/cb01-198.pdf

United States Census Bureau. (2001, December 13). *World's older population growing by unprecedented 800,000 a month*. United States Department of Commerce News Press Release. Retrieved May 25, 2002, from http://www.census.gov/Press-Release/www/2001/cb01-198.pdf

United States Equal Employment Opportunity Commission. (2000). *Charge statistics FY 1992 through FY 2000*. Retrieved August 8, 2001, from http://www.eeoc.gov/stats/charges.html

Walker, A. (1998). *Managing an ageing workforce: A guide to good practice*. Dublin, Ireland: European Foundation for the Improvement of Living and Working Conditions.

Walker, A., & Taylor, P. (1998). *Combating age barriers in employment: A European portfolio of good practice*. Luxembourg, Germany: Office for Official Publications of the European Communities.

CHAPTER THREE

Exploring Child Welfare through International Innovations

Katherine van Wormer

Barndomen kommer aldrig igen.
Childhood never comes again.

—traditional Swedish saying

Introduction

Issues related to the care of children are relatively the same the world over. It is not surprising, therefore, that programs that seem to be working well in one part of the world come to be adopted and then adapted to the needs of children somewhere else. Given this sharing of knowledge, and that from common problems come common solutions, it is sometimes difficult to pinpoint where something started. Consider, for example, the impact of the global market and international conventions. As the world grows progressively smaller through the revolution in technology, moreover, the reality of global interconnectedness extends to the daily social work scene. And one nation's experiment becomes another's standard practice.

This chapter discusses the transfer of knowledge—contemporary knowledge—pertaining to child welfare interventions. The term *child welfare* is used here not in the narrow sense of "a specialized field of practice," but in its literal meaning of the general well-being of children. The underlying assumptions of this chapter are, first, that children are the most powerless members of the human community, and secondly, that the primary source of help and nurturance for children is the family. Many families, however, cannot do the job they were meant to do, so some form of help or even substitutive care has to be provided. In societies that have formal, *residentially* based social services, intervention occurs only when there is some sort of serious failure to meet the child's needs. Under the contrasting *institutional* arrangement, on the other hand, child welfare services are largely preventative and routinely made available to all children in the society (Kadushin & Martin, 1988).

Child welfare practice is only as strong as the social welfare state on which it depends for sustenance. Policies that are sound in theory often die "on the vine" for lack of institutional support. Then those same policies are brought to fruition on more fertile ground. For example, family preservation models, which have been introduced in the United States with mixed results and serious underfunding, have become models of excellence in the Danish welfare state (see Pecora, 1992).

We begin our discussion of global exchange with a review of interventions that the U.S. has borrowed, in whole or in part, from elsewhere in the world. These innovations are in the areas of child protection and juvenile justice. In the second portion of this chapter, we explore a major ideological framework, empowerment originated theory, and a practice innovation, family preservation services, in light of their impact at home and abroad. The chapter concludes with a brief discussion of what the U.S. can learn from other countries. (To do this topic real justice would require a separate book.) There is much that can be learned from both macro-level policies that are perceived as the rights of the people, policies that range from universal health care and guaranteed income to more specialized programs. On the smaller scale, policies such as family allowances, maternity/paternity leaves, subsidized childcare and nonviolent childrearing are the most relevant. Looming over the entire subject of the treatment of children are the guiding principles included in the historic United Nations Convention the Rights of the Child. Many nations (but not the U.S. which has failed to ratify it) have taken this historic document and its human rights provisions seriously and are modifying their legislation accordingly so as to be in compliance.

Innovations Borrowed

Ensuring the welfare of children is a value espoused throughout the world (Dominelli, 1999). Abuse, neglect, and impoverishment of children are universal concerns as well. The manner of handling these concerns, however, is politically and ideologically based and reflects the value a society places on protecting its citizens of all ages. There is much to learn concerning effective child welfare practice from a study of initiatives from the various parts of the world.

In recent years, a considerable body of literature has evolved on the subject of family/child interventions: An Internet search of the Social Work Abstracts index under the keyword heading of *family/child practice* reveals 812 references (as of December 2003). When the words *child welfare* and *international* are combined, 168 articles are listed.[1] Of all the innovations described in this voluminous literature, the transfer of knowledge is chiefly from one European country to another or from the United States to a European country. Many of these programs such as universal child supports or free day care would be considered too costly by American standards.

Perhaps the U.S. is hindered by the social values of traditionalism, individualism, and a resurgent punitiveness (see van Wormer, 2004). Or perhaps the reason for American intransigence is what Senator William Fulbright (1966) once termed "the arrogance of power," the belief that American ways are the best, coupled with an indomitable distrust of foreign interference, the same distrust that keeps the U.S. as only one of two hold-outs in the world (Somalia being the other) in ratifying the United Nations Convention on the Rights of the Child.

I have identified five avenues of transference from overseas to the U.S. with special relevance to the welfare of children. These are kinship care, family group conferencing, shared family care, community services, and restorative justice.

Kinship Care

Kinship care or kinship fostering is a tradition that dates from the time of non-industrialized, non-bureaucratized societies in which care

---

1. Among the many relevant books written from a comparative perspective are (*Community Approaches to Child Welfare: International Perspectives* (Dominelli, editor, 1999); *Saving Our Children from Poverty: What the United States Can Learn From France* (Bergmann, 1996), *The Future of Child Protection* (Waldfogel, 1998), *Family Change and Family Policies in Great Britain, Canada, New Zealand, and the United States* (Kamerman & Kahn, 1997), *Canadian Family Policies* (Maureen Baker, 1995), and *Innovations in Practice and Service Delivery across the Lifespan* (Biegel & Blum, editors, 1999).

of children was a community responsibility. Adoption and formal foster care, in contrast, are modern, urban concepts with institutional arrangements centering around the nuclear family. The African tradition of kinship and communal networks has played a significant role in the survival of African Americans (Williams, 1999). Although kinship care's historical roots as an informal practice are deep, its use as a formal child welfare service is relatively new (Ingram, 1999).

As with many borrowed practices, the exact trail of the expansion of kinship foster care and adoption is unclear. Ernst (1999) traces the roots of formalized kinship care to culturally-specific practices in New Zealand. In their Family Group Conferences, the indigenous population of New Zealand, the Maori people, determined who in their community would take responsibility for the child in need of care. This practice, which was written into New Zealand law in 1989, has influenced U.S. foster care policy, according to Ernst.

In the United States in the 1980s, the idea of formalized kinship care within the child welfare system rapidly gained ground as the demand for homes in which to place needy children far exceeded the number of available registered foster homes (Ingram, 1996). The growing recognition of the benefits of family care and the stabilizing effect extended family can have on placement also contributed to the promotion of relative foster care, as did the desire by all parties to avoid placement of children outside of their own racial or ethnic communities.

Formal kinship care often involves placement with a grandmother, generally African American, generally in need of financial assistance, which is provided with this program. Key advantages of such an arrangement are its relative permanence and stability, the child's familiarity with the setting and relatives, continuity in schooling, and the absence of stigmatizing (Greef, 1999). Research indicates that children remain in kinship care 30 percent longer than children in other forms of care (Wulczyn, Harden, & George, 1997). Although this may be more costly to the state, the advantage of the stability of an extended stay in the home of caring relatives should not be overlooked. The Adoption and Safe Families Act of 1997 (P.L. No. 105-189) has called for more extensive evaluation of the use of kinship care.

There are many unanswered questions concerning state-funded kinship foster care: To what extent is financial support provided? How willingly will relatives who have cared for their nieces, nephews, and grandchildren informally accept formal supervision of their care? How can social workers be sure that the substance abuse, physical mal-treatment, or incest that existed in the parents is not endemic in the extended family as well? One thing that appears certain is that kin-ship care is here to stay, and adequate financial and psychological supports for the family are essential. For the first time, in Europe as well as the United States, the public child welfare system recognizes the rewards to all parties concerned in extended family care.

Family Group Conferencing

A more obvious example of direct international transfer of innova-tions is the introduction of family group conferences. The family group conference, which originated in New Zealand in the early 1980s from pressures exerted by the indigenous Maori community, is a forum in which family members, chosen by the child and parent, come together to take primary responsibility for developing a plan of child protec-tion (Marsh & Crow, 1998; Waldfogel, 1998). Seeing parents as part-ners rather than adversaries marks a deep contrast with traditional child protection conferences in Britain and the United States. This Maori-centered approach was based on a firm commitment to seek and support the strengths of families caught in the throes of major child welfare crisis, a crisis generally involving abuse, neglect, or de-linquency. Instead of a focus on problems in the family, the focus is on solutions (Marsh & Crow, 1998), and all participants—including children—have a voice in these meetings. Family group conferencing is now the norm in New Zealand, especially in cases of juvenile delin-quency. Institutionalized in law in 1989, most juvenile cases are di-verted by court cases generally involving abuse, neglect, or delinquency. Similarly, in Canada, family expertise is sought as a way of ensuring child care and safety. Consistent with the Canadian approach of partnering with family members, clients are viewed as colleagues in the helping process. As Wharf (1995) explains, demeaning and de-humanizing language such as "target populations," "multiproblem families," and "case management" are avoided.

About the same time that the New Zealand experiment was getting underway, the Children's Services Department in Portland, Oregon, was independently trying out a model of practices with a strong fam-ily solutions component, the family unity meeting. Although the ex-tended family was not emphasized as strongly in this model, as time has gone on, the links between the family unity meeting and the family group conferencing have grown, and more of the Conference family-centered approach has been incorporated (Marsh & Crow, 1998). In Oregon, special attention has been paid to involving the whole agency in mass educational efforts in strengths-based attitudes and policies.

Not to be outdone, the United Kingdom drew on ideas from both New Zealand and from Oregon in their interpretation of the UK Children Act of 1989. Now influenced by initiatives in other parts of the English-speaking world, family rights became more widely recognized in child welfare work. There was no equivalent reorganization of efforts in youth justice, however, despite its prominent place in New Zealand programming (Marsh & Crow).

In the 1990s, proponents from New Zealand and Australia introduced family group conferencing to North America with lectures and training workshops (Umbreit & Zehr, 1996). Thousands of law enforcement offices, judges, and school officials have since been trained. Pilot programs are proliferating. Huge backlogs of court cases and lengthy adversarial procedures have hindered child welfare decisions until the children are half grown. New laws mandating prompt and permanent resolutions within a reasonable time period combined with federal funding for court initiatives have helped create a climate ripe for experimentation. The chief judge of Jefferson County, Kentucky, for example, is giving family group conferencing a try (Spake, 1999). A major advantage of this approach is that through brainstorming by members of the community, the child invariably will remain within his or her community and not be placed in ethnically "alien" territory. The idea, which originated within a minority culture in one country, translates well to work with minorities in various parts of the globe. The reliance on the extended family, moreover, as a positive and often untapped resource is consistent with the strengths perspective of social work practice and the social work code of ethics focus on client self-determination. This client-centered approach entails a shift in assumptions about the way child welfare services are planned and delivered away from models that emphasize pathology and toward those with an understanding of family and social neutrality in the resolution of problems (Burford & Hudson, 2000).

Although rigorous outcome data are yet to be provided about the effectiveness of such conferencing in providing long-term solutions to child care problems, preliminary evaluations report active participation by all parties, clear agreement on relevant issues, and high levels of satisfaction with the process (Marsh & Crow, 1998). This radically different method of resolving child welfare issues has been adopted in Oregon, British Columbia and Alberta, Canada, Israel, Norway, Sweden, and South Africa as well as in Australia/New Zealand and the United Kingdom.

Shared Family Care

Some years a group of American professors from the University of Washington ventured to Aarhus, Denmark, to study a remarkable whole family placement program in which families with serious systematic problems receive six to eight weeks of constant supervision and guidance in their child rearing practices. Peter Pecora (1992), who described his observations in the NASW Strengthening Families through International Innovations Transfer project, was one of the participants in this exchange. And to what extent were these ideas adopted in America? According to Pecora in personal correspondence of October 24, 2000, the Shared Family Care program in Colorado Springs is one such program modeled on European concepts. An article in Colorado's *The Gazette* (Sampson, 2000) describes this remarkable program. Instead of splitting up the family while it gets help, as Sampson informs us, the local social service agency has moved entire families into foster care. Unlike Denmark's foster care arrangement in which families are mentored by professionally trained social workers, these families move in with a mentor family, hopefully to absorb parenting skills from their hosts. The beauty of this program, according to the article, is that it enables families who have minimal support systems to get the resources and skills they need to move toward self-sufficiency. This practice of opening one's home to unrelated dependent adults has been in operation for centuries in Europe (Barth, 1994).

Barth singles out five types of shared family care arrangements in the United States: residential programs for children that also offer residence and treatment for their parents, drug and alcohol treatment programs for adults that also offer treatment for children, drug treatment programs for mothers and children, residential programs for pregnant and parenting mothers, and foster family homes that offer care of parents and children. In Sweden, Barth informs us, roughly 10 percent of all children in out-of-home care are in treatment homes for adults with drug or alcohol dependency problems. Although funding for such whole-family program designs has not been as widely available in America as in Europe, this form of family presentation holds much promise for future development.

Community Services

The Patch Project in Cedar Rapids, Iowa, utilizes a model that originated in Britain in the 1970s and 1980s. This model uses a neighborhood-based interagency team to deliver child protective services, along with other child and family services (Waldfogel, 1998). The name comes from British "patch-working" which involves assigning social workers and other staff to cover a specific "patch" or neighborhood. The link between child protection and health workers and housing has been extended to include juvenile protection officers and welfare workers. Results have been positive; the neighborhood team has encouraged informal interaction between clients and workers. Another striking result, according to Waldfogel, is that team members are now less likely to cite child abuse and neglect as their clients' primary problems and more likely to cite problems such as poverty, inadequate housing, mental illness, unemployment, and substance abuse. The Patch Project is also expanding to cover five additional sites in Iowa.

Restorative Justice

When the family conferencing process described above resolves issues related to criminal acts, it is sometimes referred to as *restorative justice*. Restorative justice, the restoring of justice to the victim and the community, is an empowering, non-adversarial approach with important implications for youths in trouble with the law. At the same time that extremely harsh punishments have been meted out to juveniles who have engaged in acts of property destruction, many juvenile justice officials in the U.S. are looking to models imported from Australia, New Zealand, and Canada. These models inspired by the practices of indigenous people are now officially sanctioned in many places. In Canada, a vision of justice as peacemaking has spread from historically pacifist churches such as the Mennonite, into the mainstream of Christianity (Cayley, 1999). In Pennsylvania, the "balanced and restorative justice model" has now become law (DeVore & Gentilcore, 1999). Built on innovative practices, the Pennsylvania model meets the special needs of at-risk students while fulfilling the program's objectives of ensuring community safety, offender accountability, and competency development. Instead of being banished from the community and locked up with hardened criminals, young lawbreakers are forced to make amends to the community and to enter a rigorous educational program with a focus on character development as well as vocational competencies.

Vermont has become the first state to implement reparative boards on a statewide basis and the first to commit to institutionalize the new restorative philosophy throughout their correctional system (Marks, 1999). Through victim-offender conferencing, the victim and the community are likely to get some closure.

An enormous amount of hope and creative energy is being invested in restorative justice initiatives (van Wormer, 2001). Through workshops, judicial training sessions, law enforcement and correctional conferences, and well-publicized demonstration projects, the excitement is spreading. Preliminary research results from victim surveys indicate a high level of satisfaction with the programs (Bazemore & Umbreit 1998). Measures of recidivism rates similarly indicate that youths who have successfully completed the conferencing process are less likely to re-offend than these who go through regular probation (Marks, 1999).

The implications of this restorative framework for child welfare are dramatic. Children in trouble are children who are in danger—of running away, of illicit drug use, of joining gangs for protection, and of being victimized sexually and through other forms of violence. The lives and futures of youthful offenders can be protected by using models geared not only toward the needs of their victims, but also to their own rehabilitation.

In summary, the child welfare system in the United States has benefited from the international transfer of child welfare interventions, a transfer with the potential for much impact in the future. It is in the juvenile justice arena, however, with its sweeping, even revolutionary reforms, that the exchange of international ideas has been the most comprehensive. As of 1996, at least 10 states were engaged in redefining their mission and restructuring their activities to hold juvenile offenders accountable to their victims within the community rather than hauling the offenders off for harsh punishment for his or her involvement in crime (Umbreit & Zehr, 1996).

Innovative Programs from the U.S.

Empowerment Theory

In general, the exchange of information, like the exchange of news in the media, travels from the U.S. to other countries. Consider the effect that feminism, an outgrowth of the American Civil Rights Movement and the consciousness raising that followed, brought to bear on the world stage. Today women's shelters to protect battered women and their families and rape crisis centers are found the world over. At the ideological level, the notion of *empowerment*, which has its roots in feminist thought and writings, has come to shape the very nature of social works practice internationally (Shera & Wells, 1999). This form of practice is motivated by a social justice goal and through confronting power inequality and oppression. Paralleling the awareness of the mistreatment of women was a resurgence of interest in child protection. This interest was accompanied by the introduction of mandatory reporting laws in the late 1960s and of stepped up child protection services in the United States and Britain (Waldfogel, 1998). Over the past two decades, the discovery of the link between domestic violence against women and child abuse within the family has gained prominence in child welfare circles.

The United States is strong on ideas and on grassroots movements that form the impetus for federal legislation. From the United States also comes well-funded research from the social sciences, which informs theories relevant to the long-term effects of violence against children. The United States is strong on theory and empirically grounded research design but weak on structural supports. Empowerment-oriented services such as family preservation initiatives can only achieve limited success in the absence of a wider safety net and universal health care and welfare provisions.

Family Preservation Services

On the surface, one would think that family preservation like "family values" would entail government aid for all families with children, the minimum wage as a living wage, free or subsidized child, care for working mothers and single fathers, and universal health care/mental health care. The term *family preservation* refers to the goal enacted in the passage of the Adoption Assistance and Child Welfare Act of 1980 [PL 96-272] to reduce unnecessary out-of-home placements by providing intensive, round-the-clock services. Unfortunately, Congress did not fund the mandates of the law and a series of high profile child deaths followed. The increasing impoverishment of the families discharged from the welfare rolls and forced into jobs that often pay very low wages without adequate child care arrangements is likely to place more families with children at risk of child neglect (McGowan and Walsh, 2000).

Family preservation, according to Spake (1999), stresses keeping children in their birth families, communities, and ethnic groups. The reasoning judges use in individual cases (such as one cited by Spake where a child was forcibly removed from foster care to be returned to his birth mother, a convicted child murderer) stems in part from English common law which regarded children as property. State laws tend to emulate the English common law, making biology pre-eminent, according to this article. The British legacy prevails in Canada as well. The provinces, which like the U.S. are committed to the dictates of family preservation, are not providing enough money to ensure that families get the help they need (Jenish, 1997). In Norway and Sweden, in contrast, the interests of the child takes precedence over other considerations and all such programs are generously financed (van Wormer, 1993, 1997).

Intensive family preservation services have the potential when exported to other countries to enrich local systems, especially if these services are provided within the context of a highly advanced welfare state. The thriving whole family interventions and family conference decision making described previously are cases in point. Campbell (1998) describes how intensive family preservation services were introduced on Australian shores with some measure of success as long as families' problems were manageable.

While family preservation services in the United States have failed to do what was promised (i.e., to prevent the need for children to be placed outside the home), new initiatives are now capturing the imagination of child welfare policy makers (Littell & Schuerman, 1999). These initiatives encourage the community to take responsibility in the way child welfare problems are addressed. For example, a dual track system might have the community take responsibility in low-risk cases while child welfare agencies would serve high-risk cases (Littell & Schuerman, 1999). Human service systems are beginning to realize that consumers of services have a right to be involved in their own treatment (Kelly & Blythe, 2000).

The universal dilemma is whether to risk erring on the side of the child or on the side of the family. Perhaps the issue is not either/or but both/and as Wharf (1995) helpfully suggests. Maybe it is not an issue of whether you should protect the child or support the family but rather how to provide a means of empowerment for all persons in the equation. Such a balance can be achieved, according to Wharf, through the building of mutual aid associations and group and community approaches to provide the maximum benefit for all family members.

The principle of empowerment, discussed earlier, is the cornerstone of community-centered innovations. Carter (1997), for example, describes how African-centered family services and the use of a strengths perspective, which helps people tap into their own resources, can protect children and empower families within the natural context of their home communities. Incorporating natural networks that exist within African American communities (for example, churches and child-care cooperatives) can strengthen high-risk families and prevent removal of children by child welfare authorities.

A rare find in the literature is the description of an artificially designed community that houses 13 families, most headed by foster parents. The "village" is located on a former Air Force base in Rantoul, Illinois. Generously funded by the state of Illinois, this experiment in community living is generally considered a successful model soon expected to be emulated in Ohio and elsewhere (Henry, 2000).

Another model of child protection premised on increasing partnerships with families through community involvement is found in Iowa. Placing less emphasis on the incident in question and more on the family's strengths and concerns, social workers who work for the Iowa Department of Human Services learn strength-based assessment in workshops and trainings that are offered statewide. Instead of focusing on problem-solving, workers are encouraged to ask solution-focused questions. Questions of the form, "After all you've been through, how did you find enough strength to keep pushing on?" as opposed to "What could you have done differently?" are geared toward extracting positive rather than negative responses.

In Oregon, similarly, the casework assessments shifted from looking at problems to focusing on how to help families. The family unity meeting discussed earlier evolved as a partnership between professionals and family members. The Oregon model has many similarities with family group conferencing but developed independently of it.

Hawaii, with its universal health care and its generously funded programs, is written up in the Canadian *Globe and Mail* as the one "child welfare workers in Canada point to . . . (that the) country must replicate if it is to attack the roots of delinquency, crime . . . and wasted human potential" (Gadd, 1997, p. A1). The Hawaiian program cites an almost unbelievable success rate of 99 percent in preventing child abuse and neglect. This state funded program, called Healthy Start, is basically an early-intervention program that turns potentially bad parents into good ones. It achieves this, according to the article, "not by lecturing, punishing or advising, but by providing the nurturing care that most of them (the parents) never had."

Common to all these innovations is their reliance on the strengths/empowerment framework in working with, not against, families in the fulfillment of mutual goals. The strengths perspective is conceptualized by Saleebey (2002) and the empowerment perspective as formulated by Simon (1994) and Gutierrez and Lewis (1999) is rapidly emerging as the most powerful framework for counseling and other interventions in North America. The model is quite simple, its realization much more complex, but yet its formulation is an American offering that should serve to embrace child welfare practice internationally.

What the U.S. Can Learn from Other Countries

The United States can learn a great deal from other countries, both in terms of specific innovative programs and in terms of the broader social policies that underpin these programs. We must keep in mind, however, that innovations cannot be implemented in a social vacuum; their success depends very largely on the strength of the social welfare system of which they are a part. How can a family living in dire poverty be preserved? How can the state ensure the protection of a child when the rights of the biological family are given priority? How can neglect be prevented in the absence of affordable childcare? One would expect, in general, that a peaceful, democratic society with a strong sense of community would be a society in which the welfare of children would be paramount.

In striving to redress the balance between the rights of parents, children, and public authorities, social workers could, and should, look to international perspectives. The United Nations Convention on the Rights of the Child, which defines standards for child treatment and cements them in international law, is a logical starting point for conceptualizing how children's needs can best be met. (Some lawmakers in the U.S. view this treaty as an infringement on parents' rights and the right of the state to execute children who have committed heinous crimes; because it includes the right to have an abortion, ratification of this document by the U.S. Senate is unlikely [Macklin, 2000].)

The Convention's 30 articles cover political as well as economic and social rights and guarantee children adequate education, housing, nutrition, and health care, while protecting them from violence. By ratifying this document, national governments have not only demonstrated their commitment to protecting children's rights. They have also confirmed their willingness to be held accountable to the international community in instances where they have not heeded their responsibility in caring for children, and that they are willing to answer to international law.

Children's rights can be conceived of as a unifying concept with which to explore child welfare across borders. Taking the child's right to be protected from violence as a case in point, a number of European countries forbid all corporal punishment of children. Sweden, in 1979, was the first country to forbid this form of assault followed by Finland, Denmark, Norway, Austria, New Zealand, Cyprus, Croatia, Latvia, Italy, and Israel. The U.S., given its tradition of individualism and belief in the sanctity of the nuclear family, is a long way from providing this form of protection for children. Nationwide surveys show that 61 percent of American parents condone spanking as a regular form of punishment for young children, and that many parents have unrealistic expectations of behavior (Springen, 2000). Even the authors of *Child Welfare Services*, Kadushin and Martin (1998), make an attempt to distinguish discipline as "legitimate violence" from abuse which is viewed as excessive. This form of violence is legitimate, they argue, because of its corrective purpose. Murray Straus (1994), however, provides data from two national violence surveys to show a close correlation between physical punishment in childhood and increased risk of juvenile delinquency, spouse abuse, and criminal behavior later in life. Changing attitudes on this subject will take time; the best place to start is probably in parent education classes in high school.

The most pervasive form of abuse against children, however, comes not directly from parents, but indirectly through cruelty and punitiveness in the social order. A society in which survival-of-the-fittest rather than justice and equality has been the predominant cultural mode hardly could fail to be oppressive toward children (van Wormer, 1997).

If we are truly serious about reducing incidents of abuse and neglect, we need to address the clear connection between poverty, and abuse and neglect. As David Gil (1998), in his recent book on oppression and injustice states:

> My studies of child abuse and neglect led me to conclude that the abuse inflicted upon children by society exceeded in scope and destructive consequences their abuse and neglect by parents. . . . I also realized that abuse of children by their parents is frequently associated with abuse of the parents by society (p. 109).

The societal abuse to which Gil was referring includes unemployment, poverty, discrimination, ill-health, and work stress, events that are related to injustice and oppression. The well-being of children is directly related to the family's standard of living, to their ability to provide food, clothing, shelter, and time necessary for childcare. The well-being of children is indirectly related to parental stress inasmuch as economic and other forms of hardship are apt to be displaced onto vulnerable family members. In the U.S., the adoption in 1996 of welfare "reform," the Personal Responsibility and Work Opportunity Reconciliation Act (PL 104-193), for example, will likely cause higher levels of poverty and child neglect by forcing mothers on welfare to work (Littell & Schuerman, 1999).

The United States has a lot to learn from Europe regarding the level of welfare benefits that citizens of other countries enjoy. Whereas the model of child welfare in the U.S. is based on individual need and protection from harm by a particular family—a deficit model—broader conditions related to healthful standards of living are not a part of our national child welfare strategy. Yet as Clifton and Hodgson (1997) indicate, to honor the spirit of the CRC, the approach to child welfare needs focus on broader, preventive methods under which children can not only survive but actually flourish.

Let us now consider the ways in which many industrialized countries safeguard the interests of children by providing services to families. Noting that the U.S. has the lowest level of welfare benefits and highest rates of poverty compared to other Western industrialized countries, Ruth Sidel (1996) singles out four areas of significant universal support: universal cash benefits in the form of a family allowance given automatically to all families with children; some form of national health care; benefits for single-parent-headed households; and free or low cost excellent paternity leave benefits to allow new parents to stay home with their infants. Through such programming and a progressive income tax structure, child poverty levels are kept low—only about 2 to 5 percent in Scandinavia, for example, compared to the 22.4 percent in the U.S. (UNICEF, 2000). To this list we can add strict gun control laws protecting the lives of children—in the U.S., 10 per day die of gunshot wounds (Children's Defense Fund, 2000).

While the U.S. makes military spending a priority, other countries spend much more proportionally on the general well-being of their citizens. Some of the best preventatives for situations of child abuse and neglect may be reduction in stress on families, especially on single-parent families. All families require support through provision of health care, day care, and jobs that pay an adequate wage. One chilling example of the link between the absence of affordable child care and child homicide has been found by Dr. Richard Kaplan (2000), a pediatric forensic expert, who has observed a pattern in his child homicide investigations: The mother's boyfriend reluctantly baby-sits while she works; the boyfriend gets out of control and beats, sometimes killing, the child.

A program of parent education for all parents-to-be and a program of periodic public health nurse home visits to monitor the progress of children is invaluable in ensuring children's health. For all its talk of "family values," the United States is not a family-friendly society. In contrast, in Sweden and Norway, a year of maternity leave at near full salary is provided to ensure that one of the parents will stay home with the child. Childcare fees are set on a sliding scale and the standards of public day care are extraordinarily high. At the heart of such policies is the premise that the whole community thrives when families and children thrive. The United States would do well to look toward policies that strengthen rather than weaken the ability of vulnerable families to raise healthy children. By not catching problems early, we pay the price later in escalating crime, drug use, and spread of disease. What we must keep in mind, as Sidel (1996) observes, is that these problems are not insoluble. There are models from other countries where the rates of poverty, infant mortality and morbidity, crime and drug abuse, and child neglect and abuse are quite low, and, in short, where protection of families and children is intertwined.

For example, here is a quick checklist of just a few of the benefits France provides for its families: a monthly allowance of $600 per child starting with the second birth; paid maternity leave for a least six months; job protection for mothers, including unpaid leave up to three years; free hospital and medical care before and after birth; free daycare system and nursery care; and free education including university (Clark, 1998). We ought to look to Europe for a society that truly honors family values, as Clark wisely suggests.

Conclusion

In this chapter, we have seen how in this age of global inter-connectedness and rapid information transfer, innovations developed in one part of the world have come to be adopted and modified some-where else. Thus the U.S. has moved in the direction of kinship care as a more satisfying form of foster care than entrusting children to the care of strangers; toward restorative justice as a non-punitive form of restoring the balance between juvenile offenders and their victims; and toward family group conferencing as a collaborative form of de-cision making concerning a child in need of care. Going in the oppo-site direction, American initiatives in regard to family preservation and empowerment perspectives have been explored and emulated on the European continent. Learning about specific child welfare solu-tions to universal problems helps provide new ways of addressing children's needs in one's own country.

Of all the truths that emerged in the present discussion, perhaps the greatest was the extent to which dealing with the personal dimensions of children's lives requires a critical perspective on the social, political, and economic contexts that frame children's lives. A major argument of this chapter is that child protection has come too much to mean protection from parental harm rather than promotion of children's well being. A social system that tolerates high levels of poverty for families with children and that institutes policies requiring single parents to work in the absence of adequate child care arrangements is setting the stage for child neglect and most probably abuse. Although several of the community-oriented service innovations described in these pages are worth pursuing for the promising results they offer to some families, and child welfare workers deserve public recognition for the vital work that they do in rescuing children, such services alone cannot alter the social conditions that may have helped generate the problems in the first place.

The welfare of children in the family is tied inextricably to the welfare of families, socially and economically. To what extent the United States and other countries in similar positions will devote their resources and creative energy to real family protection, and to what extent the money will be diverted into non-family-oriented areas, remains to be seen. The key point of this chapter, generally speaking, is that a society that is good to its members will have members who are good to their children. Treat the parents well, and they will treat their children well. Kindness transcends the system, as does leanness and meanness.

References

Baker, M. (1995). *Canadian family policies*. Toronto: University of Toronto Press.

Barth, R. P. (1994) Shared family care: Child protection and family preservation. *Social Work, 39* (5). 515–524.

Bazemore, G. & Umbreit, M. (1998). Balancing the response to youth crime: Prospects for a restorative juvenile justice in the twenty-first century. In Albert Roberts (Ed.), *Juvenile justice: Policies, programs, and services* (pp 371–408). Belmont, CA: Wadsworth.

Bergmann, B.R. (1996). *Saving our children from poverty: What the United States can learn from France*. New York: Russell Sage Foundation.

Biegel, D.E. & Blum, A. (Eds.) (1999). *Innovations in practice and service delivery across the lifespan*. New York: Oxford University Press.

Burford, G. & Hudson, J. (Eds.) (2000). *Family group conferencing: New directions in community-centered child and family practice*. New York: Aldine de Gruyter.

Campbell, L. (1998). Translating intensive family preservation services across national boundaries: An Australian experience. *Child Welfare, 67,* 79–93.

Carter, C.S. (1997). Using African-centered principles in family preservation services. *Families in Society 78,* 531–538.

Cayley, D. (1999, March 27). Applause, please, for the new tack on young lawbreakers. *Globe and Mail,* D3.

Children's Defense Fund (2000). *The state of America's children yearbook 2000.* Washington DC: Children's Defense Fund, D3.

Clarke, K. (1998, May). My French whine about family values. *U.S. Catholic 63*(5), 26–27.

Clifton, J. & Hodgson, D. (1997). Rethinking practice through a children's rights perspective. In C. Cannan & C. Warren (eds.), *Social action with children and families.* (pp 43–65). London: Routledge

DeVore, D. & Gentilcore, K. (1999). Balanced and restorative justice and educational programming for youth at risk. *The Clearing House 73*(2), 96–108.

Dominelli, L. (Ed.). (1999). *Community approaches to child welfare: International perspectives.* Aldershot, England: Ashgate.

Ernst, J.S. (1999). Whanau knows best: Kinship care in New Zealand. In R. Hegar & M Scannapieco (Eds.), *Kinship foster care: Policy, practice, and research.* (Chap. 8) New York: Oxford University Press.

Fulbright, J.W. (1966). *The arrogance of power.* New York: Vintage Books.

Gadd, J. (1997, October 18). Paradise found for child welfare. *The Globe and Mail,* A1.

Gil, D. (1998). *Confronting injustice and oppression.* New York: Columbia University Press.

Greeff, R. (1999). Kinship, fostering, obligations, and the state. In R. Greeff (Ed.), *Fostering kinship: An international perspective on kinship foster care.* (pp 17–19). Altershot, England: Ashgate Publishing.

Gutierrez, L.M. & Lewis, E. A. (Eds.). (1999). *Empowering women of color. New York: Columbia University Press.*

Henry, E. (1997, May). Homes for foster children. *Kiplinger's Personal Finance Magazine 51*(5), 143–144.

Ingram, C. (1999). Kinship care: From last resort to first choice. *Child Welfare, 75,* 550–566.

Jenish, D'Archy (1997, April 14). Too many tears: The news about abused kids just keeps getting worse. *Maclean's, 110*(15), 18–20.

Kadushen, A. & Martin, J. (1988). *Child welfare services,* (4th ed.). New York: Macmillan.

Kamerman, S. & Kahn, A. (Eds.). (1997). *Family change and family policies in Great Britain, Canada, New Zealand, and the United States.* London: Oxford University Press.

Kaplan, R. (2000, October 5). *Child abuse investigations in Iowa.* Guest lecture at the University of Iowa, Cedar Falls.

Kelly, S. & Blythe, B. (2000). Family preservation: A potential not yet realized. *Child Welfare, 79,* (1), 29–42.

Littell, J.H. & Schuerman, J.R. (1999). Innovations in child welfare: Preventing out-of-home placement of abused and neglected children. In D.E. Biegel & A. Blum (Eds.). *Innovations in practice and service delivery across the lifespan.* (pp. 102–123). New York: Oxford University Press.

Macklin, W.R. (2000, January 28). 300,000 children being exploited for military purposes. Knight-Ridder/Tribune News Service, KO153.

Marks, A. (1999, September 8). Instead of jail, criminals face victims. *Christian Science Monitor,* 1, 4.

Marsh, P. & Crow, G. (1998). *Family group conferences in child welfare.* Oxford, England: Blackwell Science.

Pecora, P. (1992, January 29). (Ed.). *The NASW strengthening families through international innovations transfer project.* Unpublished report submitted to NASW, Office of Peace and International Affairs.

Sampson, O. (2000, October 1). Foster family plan expected to spread. Available at wysiwyg://132/http://www.gazette.com/archive/00-10-01/daily/top1a.html.

Saleebey, D. (2002) (Ed) The strengths perspective in social work practice, 3rd edition. New York: Longman.

Shera, W. & Wells, L.M. (1999 (Eds.) *Empowerment practice in social work: Developing richer conceptual foundations.* Toronto: Canadian Scholars' Press.

Sidel, R. (1996). *Keeping women and children last: America's war on the poor.* New York: Penguin books.

Simon, B.L. (1994). *The empowerment tradition in American social work: A history.* New York: Columbia University Press.

Spake, A. (1999, April 19). Judge push to get kids into stable homes. *U.S. News and World Report 126* (15), 62–63.

Springen, K. (2000, October 16). On spanking. *Newsweek,* 64.

Straus, M. (1994). *Beating the devil out of them: Corporal punishment in American families.* New York: Lexington Books.

Turnell, A. & Edwards, S. (1999). Child protection: A global perspective. In A. Turnell, S. Edwards, and I.K. Berg, *Signs of Safety* (pp. 11–28). WW Norton & Co.: New York.

Umbreit, M. & Zehr, H. (1996). Restorative family group conferences: Differing models and guidelines for practice. *Federal Probation 60* (3), 24–30.

United Nations Children's Fund (UNICEF). (2000). *The state of the world's children.* New York: UNICEF.

van Wormer, K. (2004). *Confronting oppression and restoring justice: From policy analysis to social action.* Alexandria, VA: CSWE.

van Wormer, K. (2001). *Counseling female offenders and victims: A strengths-restorative approach.* New York: Springer.

van Wormer, K. (1997). *Social welfare: A world view.* Belmont, CA: Wadsworth.

Waldfogel, J. (1998). *The future of child protection.* Cambridge, MA: Harvard University Press.

Wharf, B. (1995). Toward a new vision for child welfare in Canada. *Child welfare 74,* 820–839.

Williams, J. (1999). Kinship in foster care in New York State: An African-American perspective. In R. Greef (Ed.), *Fostering kinship: An international perspective on kinship foster care.* (pp. 153–166). Aldershot, England: Ashgate Publishing, Limited.

Wulczyn, F. Harden, R. & George, A. (1997). *Foster care dynamics (1983–1994): An update from the multistate foster care data archive.* Chicago, IL: Chapin Hall Center for Children, University of Chicago.

CHAPTER FOUR

Individual Retirement Accounts, Privatization and Social Security: International Experiences

James Midgley

It is widely believed that the American social security system is on the verge of collapse and that it will soon be unable to meet the income security needs of the elderly and others in need. Commercially managed individual retirement accounts offer a viable alternative to social security. After assuming office in January 2001, President George W. Bush appointed a commission to make recommendations for establishing retirement accounts of this kind. If implemented, the president's proposal will partially privatize the nation's social security system by diverting a proportion of social security payroll contributions to individual retirement accounts. Although this proposal will not abolish social security, it is controversial and likely to face vigorous opposition. Many Democrats and lobbying groups representing the interests of elderly people have vowed to oppose partial privatization. On the other hand, the commercial insurance and pension industry is in favor of the proposal as are many Republicans and neo-liberal economists.

As the debate on private individual retirement accounts gathers momentum, the experiences of other countries that have already introduced accounts of this kind can help reveal the advantages as well as disadvantages of this approach. This chapter examines developments in three countries where individual retirement accounts have already been established. The first is Chile, where the government replaced the country's social insurance system with commercially managed retirement accounts in 1981. The second is Singapore, where individual retirement accounts managed by the government rather than commercial firms have been used to provide income protection for the elderly for many years. The third country is Britain, where the public and private retirement systems have long been articulated, and where private accounts designed to augment rather than replace the social insurance system have been introduced. These countries offer valuable lessons for the United States as the future of its social security system is being considered.

Social Security and Individual Retirement Accounts

Social security programs funded through what is known as the social insurance approach have been established in many countries. Social insurance is based on "income pooling" and the collective sharing of risk. In other words, payroll tax contributions paid by workers and their employers are used to meet contingencies which interrupt, diminish, or terminate income, creating insecurity and increasing the risk that workers and their families will fall into poverty and face serious deprivation. These contingencies include sickness, injuries at the work place, disability, maternity, unemployment, death and, of course, retirement (International Labour Office, 1984).

Although the first social insurance programs were introduced in Europe at the end of the 19th century, these programs expanded throughout the world during the middle decades of the 20th century (Dixon, 1999). At the time, many experts believed that social security offered a modern and effective solution to the problem of income insecurity. Organizations such as the International Labor Office, the International Social Security Association and the United Nations persuaded many governments to establish social insurance programs. Many political leaders and national governments welcomed these initiatives and allocated resources to promote their expansion. Many were optimistic that social insurance would end the hazard of income insecurity associated with modern life (Cockburn, 1980).

Despite its popularity, social insurance came under critical scrutiny during the 1970s. Some economists claimed that social insurance had reduced the savings rate, thereby reducing investments and impeding economic growth (Feldstein, 1974, 1977). Others argued that as the proportion of the elderly population of the industrial countries increased, social security costs would rise and create a heavy and unfair burden on those who remained economically active (Ferrara, 1982; Peterson & Howe, 1988; Peterson, 1996). Some suggested that social insurance was creating complacency and harming incentives and self-reliance. People were no longer required to meet their own income needs, and they were becoming increasingly dependent on the government (Freeman, 1981; Murray, 1984). As taxation levels increased during the 1970s, and as many countries experienced recession and other economic difficulties, these arguments gained support. Eventually, they undermined the consensus which had characterized social security policy, and by the 1980s, alternative approaches were being proposed.

Individual Retirement Accounts

Commercially-managed individual retirement accounts have been recommended as alternatives to social insurance. This proposal, which has gained considerable support since the 1980s, requires governments to mandate workers to establish savings accounts with commercial providers. Salary deductions are paid into these accounts on a regular basis and cannot be withdrawn until workers reach retirement age. Workers are permitted to invest their savings in equities and other financial products, and they may switch between commercial providers to maximize their rates of return. When they retire, they may withdraw their accumulation and spend or invest it as they wish. Alternatively, they may purchase an annuity to ensure that they have an adequate income to meet their old age retirement needs.

Advocates of individual retirement accounts believe that these accounts have many advantages over the social insurance approach (Blahous, 2000; Feldstein, 1998; Ferrara, 1982; World Bank, 1994). They contend that if workers are permitted to invest their social insurance contributions in stocks and other approved financial products, they will receive far higher returns than the benefits paid by conventional social insurance programs. The booming stock market of the 1990s, they claim, would have provided very generous rates of return. They also argue that individual retirement accounts enhance individual responsibility and self-reliance. Workers have full control over their contribution and are responsible for making investment decisions. Also, instead of having to share their contributions with others, they receive the full benefits of their investment. This encourages self-reliance and enhances individual responsibility. In addition, the burden of payroll taxation is reduced and, because more capital is available for investment, economic growth will be stimulated. Government's role will be reduced to one of regulating the commercial retirement system and providing means-tested social assistance benefits to those who cannot participate in the system. By curtailing the government's role, ordinary citizens will become more self-reliant and this will, in turn, strengthen the economy.

Opponents of privatized accounts believe that the income pooling approach which characterizes social insurance is a more effective way of providing income protection (Baker & Weisbrot, 1999; Ball, 2000; Beattie & McGillvray, 1995; Kinsgon & Williamson, 1998; Skidmore, 1999). Many individuals, they argue, will simply not be able to save enough to cover their own retirement. Women are particularly disadvantaged because their incomes tend to be lower than those of men. Also, because many leave the labor force to have children, their lifetime contributions are often inadequate to meet their retirement income needs. Because social insurance pools resources, it is able to support these women as well as other people who have low incomes. This redistributive element also promotes a sense of collective caring, and thus promotes social solidarity.

Many opponents of private individual retirement accounts are concerned that the high rates of return generated by the buoyant stock market of the late 1990s may not be sustained. A recession could, they claim, wipe out the savings of hard working people, causing many to fall into poverty in old age. They point out that social insurance has been an effective antipoverty program. Indeed, many elderly people would now be living below the poverty level if the program had not been created. The use of the private market to provide income protection is an unproven and risky strategy. It is equally risky to allow people to speculate on the stock market when few have the experience to do so prudently. Past experience with commercial providers suggests that great care is needed to protect people's savings.

The Bush Proposals

Proposals to create individual retirement accounts in the United States are not new, but they gained momentum during the 2000 presidential election campaign. As the Republican candidate, then-Governor George W. Bush promised to "save" social security for future generations by permitting a proportion of the social security contribution to be diverted into a private individual retirement account. Specifically, he proposed that 2 percent of the 12.6 percent payroll contribution be diverted to individual retirement accounts. Then-Vice President Al Gore, the Democratic candidate, opposed this proposal, contending that claims about the imminent collapse of social security were exaggerated. He promised, if elected, to take steps to ensure the program's long-term survival. However, he agreed that individual retirement accounts had a role to play, and he proposed that these accounts be introduced in addition to the existing social security system through imposing additional payroll contributions.

Following the election, President Bush moved quickly to implement his partial privatization proposal, and in May 2001 he appointed a 16-member commission to make recommendations for establishing commercially managed retirement accounts. The Commission to Strengthen Social Security, as it was known, was not asked to debate the issue, but to consider how and when these accounts could be introduced. Although the commission included both Democrats and Republicans, all supported the President's proposals (*San Francisco Chronicle*, 2001).

Democrats condemned the commission's appointment, contending that it is politically biased and likely to lead to the total privatization of social security. House Minority Leader Dick Gephart expressed his surprise that the President would advocate investing social security contributions in the stock market at a time when it was particularly vulnerable. Other Democrats echoed this sentiment and promised to oppose the commission's recommendations should proposals for the partial privatization of the system be sent to Congress (*San Francisco Chronicle*, 2001).

In July 2001, the commission announced that the social security system would be unable to meet its obligations by the year 2016. Previous estimates, which were based on very conservative assumptions about population growth and economic performance, had predicted that the system would remain solvent until 2030. The commission predictably endorsed the president's proposal and urged that it be implemented as soon as possible. The magazine *Business Week* (2001) reported that the president and his staff intended to mount a massive public relations campaign during the latter half of 2001 to garner political support for the proposal. However, the tragic events of September 11th and a sharp decline in the value of stocks effectively halted the administration's plans to proceed with the partial privatization of the social security system. It is likely that these proposals will be resurrected if President Bush is re-elected in 2004.

International Experiences

President Bush's proposal will, if implemented, fulfill the aspirations of those who have long deprecated the involvement of government in social welfare. Libertarians, traditionalists, and free-marketeers all believe that the government has no role to play in providing income protection. This belief is inspired by a deep ideological distaste for state intervention in social and economic life. Opponents of government involvement argue that individuals should be responsible for their own welfare and that their social needs, and those of their families, should be met through individual effort and the purchase of goods and services through the market.

However, most reasonable people would agree that ideological beliefs should be tempered by real world experiences, to determine whether their practical application does, in fact, promote the overriding objective of meeting social needs. The experiences of other countries can be helpful in this regard. Privatization and the creation of individual retirement accounts are not innovations unique to the United States. As was suggested earlier, the experiences of several other countries that have already experimented with these proposals can inform discussions on the future of social security in this country. Their experiences should be examined and heeded.

Chile

In 1981, Chile became the first country in the world to replace its social insurance system with a system of commercially owned and managed individual retirement accounts. Ironically, Chile was also the first country outside Europe to introduce social insurance. The Chilean government created the country's first social insurance program in 1911. But unlike Britain and the United States, different social insurance funds for different categories of workers were established. This resulted in an unwieldy administrative system, waste, inequities between the funds, and other inefficiencies (Wolfe, 1968; Mesa-Lago, 1978). Although various Chilean governments sought to consolidate the funds into a unitary system, these efforts were not successful. Many agreed that there was a critical need for reform. But few would have predicted that the reform of the Chilean system would have resulted in its total privatization.

The Chilean social security system was privatized by the military regime of General Augusto Pinochet, which overthrew the country's elected socialist government in a bloody military coup in 1973. Social security privatization was an integral part of the regime's commitment to eradicate socialist influences and to promote individualism and free enterprise. In addition to widespread human rights abuses, other measures designed to promote this goal included the suppression of the trades unions, the repeal of wage and employment agreements, and the abolition of the country's labor courts (Borzutsky, 1991).

Privatization was authorized by Decree no. 3500 of 1981. The Decree replaced the old social insurance funds with new commercially owned funds. Currently, twelve commercial funds compete to attract, manage, and invest worker's contributions. Workers are permitted to move their accounts between the funds in order to maximize their rates of return. The government regulates the funds and has established investment guidelines. Workers pay 10 percent of their wages into their accounts up a defined maximum. Additional contributions are levied to cover disability, survivor's, and health insurance. Contributions may not be withdrawn until workers reach age 60. At this time, they may choose to purchase an annuity or to receive their accumulation in regular annual installments. The funds charge a management fee for their services. Employers are totally exempt from paying contributions (Borzutsky, 1997; Edwards, 1998; Gillion & Bonilla, 1992).

The privatization of the Chilean system has been widely acclaimed and many other Latin American countries have since emulated it. Supporters believe that the Chilean social security system is now more efficient than the old insurance system. Because the funds are governed by the market, they are compelled to provide high quality services if they are to retain their members. The proponents of privatization also claim that workers now benefit from higher rates of return. Indeed, rates of return during the 1980s were favorable, averaging between 12 percent and 14 percent per year. However, during the 1990s, rates of return fell sharply to about 2 percent in the mid-1990s (*The Economist*, 1998). In addition, the high administrative charges imposed by the funds further reduced the rates of return, especially for lower-income workers (Mesa-Lago, 1994). James (1997) points out that administrative charges have reduced rates of return by as much as 5 percent.

Consequently, benefit levels have not been as high as expected. The problem is compounded by the fact that many workers with low incomes do not save enough to receive adequate pensions. This is especially true of women who leave employment to raise children. Another problem is that many Chilean workers default on paying their contributions, and many avoid payment altogether. Queisser (1995) reports that only 57 percent of workers contribute regularly and in certain occupations, such as domestic work and agriculture, participation rates are even lower.

Contribution avoidance, low wages which limit the value of contributions, and declining investment yields mean that many workers are not accumulating sufficient funds to meet their retirement needs. Indeed, many are already experiencing hardship, and Chile's current social democratic government has been compelled to subsidize the incomes of many retired people. In addition to using government revenues to establish a guaranteed minimum pension that supplements inadequate benefits, social assistance is also used to support the elderly poor who do not belong to the system (Borzutsky, 1997).

Despite the prediction that many Chilean people would meet their own retirement income needs through the market, the system has been extensively subsidized by the government. In addition to the costs of paying minimum pensions and providing social assistance, the transition costs of creating the system have been substantial. In 1981, the members of the old insurance funds were permitted to remain in the system if they wished, and some, especially those who were nearing retirement, chose to do so. However, since more than 80 percent of workers joined the new system, the resources previously generated by their payroll taxes to meet the benefits of those who had already retired were lost. Consequently, the government has been compelled to use its general revenues to pay these benefits.

Continuous government involvement has meant that the costs of maintaining the system remain high. When the new system was introduced in 1981, the military government promised that the fiscal burden of subsidizing the old social insurance system would end, and that this would result in lower taxes and ultimately in improved economic performance. Although public costs have fallen from 8 percent of GDP in 1970 to about 6 percent in 1995, they remain comparatively high. These costs are far higher than what the military regime originally predicted. Also, it is estimated that they will rise in the future (Borzutsky, 2001; *The Economist*, 1998).

Far from minimizing state involvement, substantial public revenues have been used to meet the transition costs of privatization, to subsidize inadequate pensions and to supplement the private system with social assistance payments. The government's regulation of the system is also quite extensive. It is ironic that the government of Chile has continued to play such an active role in creating, supplementing, and supporting a system that was supposed to meet the income security needs of the elderly through profit driven, market provisions.

Singapore

During the 1950s, as the epoch of European global imperialism gradually came to an end, the British government established what were known as provident funds in many of its overseas colonial territories (Dixon, 1982). These funds created mandatory retirement savings accounts for those in regular wage employment. Because the colonies were poor and largely agrarian, British colonial officials believed that social insurance was not an appropriate way of providing income protection to the elderly. However, they believed that those in regular employment should be required to save a proportion of their incomes to provide a modicum of income protection in old age. Those in the peasant economy or in the urban informal sector would have to rely on their families and other traditional forms of support until the economies of their countries were sufficiently developed to permit the introduction of social insurance (Cockburn, 1980; Midgley, 1984).

The Central Provident Fund (CPF) was introduced by the British colonial authorities in the city-state of Singapore in 1955. Unlike similar funds established in other parts of the British empire at the same time, it has since expanded significantly to cover the vast majority of the population. It has also attracted widespread interest because it has been efficiently managed and used by the government to aid its development efforts. The CPF has played a vital role in the country's economic and social development and particularly in funding its ambitious housing program (Sherraden, Nair, Vasoo, & Ngiam, 1995; Sherraden, 1997; Vasoo & Lee, 2001).

Originally, contribution rates of 10 percent were levied on both workers and employers, but these were subsequently increased, and currently amount to 18.5 percent for employees and 21.5 percent for workers. The accumulations are managed and invested by the government. On reaching retirement age, workers withdraw their accumulation in a lump sum. Although the CPF was originally intended to provide retirement benefits, the government modified the program in 1968 to permit the early withdrawal of savings to purchase a home. This was a carefully reasoned policy decision. At the time, Singapore was investing extensively in manufacturing, and the government was anxious that its workers be adequately housed. This policy complemented the government's strategy of attracting international investment and of investing its own resources in infrastructure and key strategic industries.

As a result of this decision, housing and social security policy in Singapore are now closely linked. Home ownership, usually of an apartment, is not only viewed as a means of meeting the need for shelter, but is regarded as an asset that provides income security in retirement. Home ownership is also linked to kinship obligations. In traditional Singaporean culture, children are expected to provide for their elderly parents. However, the possession of a home reinforces this cultural bond. As Singapore's former Prime Minister, Lee Kuan Yew (2000), points out, the responsibility of caring for the elderly is thus borne primarily by the family and not by the state. The CPF has also played a vital role in promoting stakeholding and solidarity. It has also fostered political stability and social integration in a diverse, multi-ethnic society.

In the mid-1990s, the CPF had about $52 billion in accumulations (Sherraden, 1997). However, it appears that the inflow of contributions into the fund is matched by withdrawals. In addition to providing retirement benefits and capital for housing, members may now withdraw accumulations to pay for higher education, medical care, and even to invest in the stock market. Although withdrawals for this latter purpose are not substantial, they have become more popular in recent years, and it is not clear how sluggish stock market performance will affect future accumulations and ultimately the retirement incomes of members.

While it is true, as Sherraden (1997) points out, that the next generation of Singaporeans will inherit substantial assets in the form of housing, cash balances and even equities, there are concerns about whether the CPF will be able adequately to meet the future retirement needs of a rapidly aging population. While many elderly people still rely on their children to support them, it is questionable whether family members can continue to provide for elderly people, and whether the provident fund will be an effective way of reinforcing familial commitments. Falling birth rates, higher mobility and a possible weakening of traditional cultural obligations to care for parents may exacerbate the problem. In the future, accumulations may not be sufficient to meet retirement income needs and, in this situation, the payment of lump sum retirement benefits may not be the best approach.

Labor shortages that attract increasing numbers of immigrants to Singapore compound the problems (Vasoo & Lee, 2001). It appears that contribution avoidance among immigrants has become an issue. As in other countries, women accumulate fewer savings than men; in addition, while the majority of women marry, there is no guarantee that they will continue to do so. If a significant proportion of Singaporeans cannot in the future accumulate sufficient funds in their provident fund accounts to meet their retirement income needs, the government will be compelled to make greater use of social assistance supplements. It may even be tempted to introduce social insurance to provide a guaranteed retirement income for all.

Britain

Until the late 19th century, life expectancy in Britain and other European countries was low, and not many people survived to old age. Of those that did, responsibility for their care was traditionally assigned to the family. The Poor Laws, introduced during the reign of Queen Elizabeth I, catered for the few who survived into old age and had no means of support. As life expectancy increased, and as the ability of family members to care for the elderly weakened, new measures were required. The first measure of this kind was the Old Age Pension Act of 1908, which was based on a means-tested, social assistance approach. Although a social insurance program to cover sickness and unemployment was introduced in 1911, it was not until 1946 that retirement income protection was introduced as a part of the country's new universal social insurance system (Glennerster, 1995).

The 1946 legislation was inspired by the famous Beveridge report of 1942 which was named after its chairman, William Beveridge. The report proposed the introduction of a comprehensive range of social service provisions designed to ensure that the basic needs of the population were met. These recommendations were accepted by the Labour government which was elected with a large parliamentary majority in 1945. In addition to creating new housing, education and health care programs, the social insurance provisions of the 1911 legislation were extended in 1946 to include old age retirement, work injury, maternity leave, and death (Hills, Ditch & Glennerster, 1994). This program, known as the National Insurance Scheme, was, in many ways, similar to the social security program introduced in the United States in 1935.

The Beveridge report recommended the creation of a social insurance program that would provide a basic, guaranteed retirement income for the elderly. Since this basic benefit could not comfortably meet all the income security needs of the elderly, the report urged that it be supplemented by private savings, family support, occupational pensions and, if necessary, by social assistance. When the National Insurance Scheme was introduced by the Labour Government in 1946, flat rate benefits providing a minimum retirement income were introduced (Glennerster, 1995). Despite the popularity of the new program, many on the left of the Labour Party believed that the Beveridge proposals were too meager. They urged the creation of a much more comprehensive and generous state-managed system which would ensure that elderly people would be publicly supported. They also hoped that private occupational pensions, which catered largely to the middle class, would be replaced by government provisions. Private pensions, they argued, reinforced the privileges and inequalities of the British class system and should be abolished.

Members of the left of the Labour Party continued to press their case, but it was only in the 1970s that their proposals were partially implemented. At the time, the Labour government recognized that the flat rate benefits paid under the 1946 National Insurance Scheme did not meet the needs of elderly people who had no savings or who were not members of a private occupational scheme. Accordingly, a second-tier pension known as the State Earnings-Related Pension Scheme (SERPS) was created. However, instead of abolishing private pensions as the left had hoped, the new program recognized their value and permitted workers in approved private occupational pension funds to opt out of SERPS. While all workers would remain in the basic National Insurance Scheme, many would be exempt from contributing to SERPS. This provision effectively institutionalized a managed, pluralist approach to retirement income protection which has remained a key feature of British social security policy since the 1970s (Glennerster, 1995).

Although many regarded this pluralist arrangement as desirable, Mrs. Thatcher's Conservative government, which was elected in 1979, declared its opposition to state involvement in income protection. In 1980, it delinked the basic National Insurance pension from consumer prices, reducing its value substantially. It also undertook a major review of the social insurance system, and proposals for greater privatization were discussed. Although some members of the Conservative government hoped to abolish the social insurance retirement system altogether, they faced strong public opposition. Instead of proceeding with their plans to repeal social insurance, they introduced measures which would gradually undermine the program and foster greater privatization (Glennerster, 1995).

In addition to reducing the value of benefits, the Conservative government created generous tax incentives for members of the SERPS program to switch to the private sector. Private personal pensions, which had previously been purchased by only a small proportion of the population, were now vigorously marketed by insurance firms, and consequently many people left the SERPS program. The formula governing the value of SERPS benefits was also changed, reducing its value and creating additional incentive to leave the program. One widely condemned modification was the abolition of a SERPS provision that compensated women who spent periods out of employment to raise children (Walker, 1998).

Walker (1998) estimates that about six million workers left the SERPS program, and are now covered by personal pension plans. However, the promotion of privatization was accompanied by a major scandal involving the misrepresentation of products and the defrauding of workers by commercial sales personnel. Evans (1998) estimates that some 400,000 people were affected and that many of these cases are still being reviewed for compensation. In addition, the public's confidence in the viability of occupational pensions was severely shaken by the Mirror Group scandal when it was discovered that the firm's pension fund had been pilfered by its owner, Mr. Robert Maxwell. Many critics have also pointed out that the costs to taxpayers of promoting privatization through incentives and tax benefits has been considerable. Walker (1998) estimates that these costs amount to about 16 billion pounds sterling (or about $22 billion).

During the 1997 general election, the Conservative Party promised that, if re-elected, it would completely privatize the social insurance retirement system. This proposal was not popular with voters and contributed to the party's humiliating defeat. However, the landslide election of the Labour Party did not, as some hoped, result in a major reversal of Conservative policies. Prime Minister Blair and his cabinet were very concerned about accusations that they would be a tax-and-spend government and, in an effort to reduce public spending, they were extremely reluctant to expand social programs. After considerable internal debate, the Labour government agreed to address the pressing issue of declining pension benefit levels. By the time of the election, the value of the basic National Insurance pension had fallen to 16 percent of average earnings. About seven million elderly people had no other income and many required social assistance supplements. Only half of all retired people qualified for the full retirement benefit. Of those who did not qualify, most were women who had been unable to contribute sufficiently over their working lives to receive the full pension.

In response to this problem, the government agreed to introduce a guaranteed minimum pension to be set at 20 percent of average earnings. However, it also decided that the private market had a major role to play in providing income security for the elderly. In a consultative document published in 1998, the Labour government reaffirmed its commitment to the basic National Insurance Scheme and agreed that its value would be linked to earnings. However, it decided to abolish SERPS and replace it with a new second-tier public pension system, to be known as the State Second Pension or SSP. This new program would cater for workers who have no occupational or private personal pension, and would pay an additional flat rate rather than earnings-related benefits. Recently, a new commercially managed individual retirement account, known as the Stakeholder Pension, has also been introduced to augment the public system. It is strictly regulated by the government and limits the administrative charges that can be imposed by providers.

The British retirement system now comprises different public and private programs. Although it may be criticized for being complicated and fragmented, it enshrines a commitment to what the Labour government calls a "flourishing public-private partnership," which it believes can deliver substantial increases in living standards for pensioners (Hewitt, 1999, p. 160). Unlike the old left of the Labour Party, which hoped for the abolition of the private pensions, and the right of the Conservative Party, which hoped for the abolition of public provisions, "New Labour" has created a system which mixes and matches the two within a coordinated, and regulated system. The debate on whether the mix has found an acceptable balance between the public and private domains will, no doubt, continue.

Privatization and Retirement Accounts: Lessons from Other Countries

Although attention has focused on Chile, Singapore and Britain, other countries have also introduced retirement accounts in both the private and public sectors, and the use of commercial provisions to meet the income needs of retired people is commonplace. Many Latin American countries have replicated the Chilean experiment with privatization. Provident funds, similar to the Singaporean CPF have been created in many Anglophone developing countries. China has introduced a unique mix of social insurance and publicly managed individual retirement accounts. The British policy of mixing public and private provisions is not unique. Many European and other industrialized nations, including Canada, Australia, and the United States, have similar systems, but the British experience of regulation and managed pluralism is particularly instructive.

Although the experiences of all of these countries can inform future policy making in the United States, the lessons discussed here will be drawn primarily from the three case studies presented. The most important of these lessons involve questions about the advantages and disadvantages of privatization, the role of individual accounts in providing retirement income protection and the proper balance between public and private provision.

On the issue of privatization, the Chilean experience suggests that commercially managed accounts can generate high rates of return to workers when the economy is strong. It also shows that those with relatively high incomes do benefit from a system of this kind. However, the costs to contributors are high because of the costly administrative charges imposed by commercial providers. These charges are needed not only to manage the funds, but to secure adequate profits for their owners and, more controversially, to meet the costs of advertising and other incentives to entice workers to switch between funds. Costs of this kind do not occur in social insurance programs.

The Chilean privatization experience reveals that fund performance is very susceptible to economic cycles. Despite government regulations designed to avoid investment risk, the high rates of return recorded in the 1980s have not been sustained. This has created major concerns about the ability of the privatized system to provide adequate retirement income protection for Chilean workers, and particularly for those with relatively low incomes. Detractors of privatization have emphasized this problem, but it is countered by those who claim that a long-term rather than short-term view of the benefits of the equity market is needed.

Perhaps the most important lesson to take from Chilean privatization is that the creation of a commercial retirement system does not obviate the need for government involvement. The transition costs of privatizing the Chilean system were high and these costs have largely been borne by taxpayers. The problem is exacerbated by the fact that the government continues to subsidize the system. The government has also agreed to underwrite the accounts of contributors if any of the commercial funds should default. The prospect that taxpayers will be required to meet the high costs of a major collapse, such as that which characterized the savings and loan scandal in the United States, is a troubling one.

Privatization in Britain, under both the Conservative and the Labour governments, has also involved substantial public costs. The Conservative government makes extensive use of tax incentives and subsidies to facilitate the purchase of private personal pensions. The Stakeholder pensions recently established by the Labour government also offer generous tax advantages to those who purchase them. The costs of these incentives are, of course, borne by taxpayers.

The case of Singapore suggests that retirement accounts do play a positive role in meeting the income security needs of the elderly. Although the Singaporean system is publicly managed, its experience shows that retirement accounts, whether in the public or private

domain, can accumulate savings that benefit ordinary people. However, despite its obvious success, family support remains crucial to the
Singaporean system and that the country's high level of economic development and generally egalitarian income distribution helps to ensure that few elderly people fall below the poverty level. Concerns
have been expressed about the ability of the system to provide adequate retirement incomes in the future. If more immigrants enter the
country and if family obligations change, the problem may become
more severe.

Since there is no redistributive mechanism in either the Singaporean
or Chilean individual account system, contributors must accumulate
sufficient savings to meet their own retirement income needs. The
Chilean case makes it clear that many low income workers, and women
in particular, are not able to do so. The problem of low contribution
levels is compounded by contribution avoidance. The fact that government needs to provide social assistance benefits to a substantial
proportion of elderly Chilean people questions the viability of this
approach.

On the issue of an appropriate public and private mix in social
security, the British experience suggests that it is possible to utilize
commercial provisions in conjunction with a universal social insurance system that provides a safety need for all. Although social assistance payments are needed to supplement the pensions of low income
elderly people, attempts to augment the system with a second-tier state
pension, as well as private provisions, has helped to ease the problem.
It is unfortunate that the Thatcher government reduced the value of
social insurance benefits and undermined the system in other ways,
thus weakening the public-private partnership. The Labour government's efforts to enhance the public system while consolidating the
partnership will not be commended by all, but it is an attempt to
strengthen social insurance and create a viable mix of private and
public provision.

Policy debates about privatization and the role of individual retirement accounts in the United States should take account of the experiences of other countries. While there may be a role for individual
retirement accounts, they need not be created at the expense of the
basic social security system. To divert a portion of social insurance
contributions to these accounts will undermine the social insurance
system and create problems similar to those encountered in Chile. As

in Chile, it is likely that substantial public spending will be needed to privatize and subsidize the system and to provide increased social assistance benefits to those who do not have sufficient retirement incomes. If the redistributive provisions of the current system are weakened, the numbers of poor elderly people will increase.

Few would deny that concerns about the long-term viability of social security need to be addressed, and proposals to shore up the system have already been formulated by respected social security experts (Baker & Weisbrot, 1999; Graetz & Mashaw, 1999; Kingson & Williamson, 1998; Steuerle & Bakija, 1994). Instead of impairing and ultimately dismantling a popular social program that has served the American people for decades, the government would do well to augment it with a more coherent, plural system of provision in which social insurance provisions are articulated with social assistance, private occupational pensions and individual retirement accounts. The private occupational pensions provided by many firms need to be strengthened, and various asset accumulation arrangements, such as the IRA, 401(k) and 403(b) provisions, which are currently permitted by the tax code, should be promoted and consolidated. These are now widely used by middle class people. Stronger incentives are also needed to increase their utilization by those with lower incomes, and greater efforts to streamline and coordinate these different forms of income protection are needed. In this way, the long-term income security of millions of Americans can be effectively promoted.

References

Baker, D. & Weisbrot, M. (1999). *Social security: The phony crisis*. Chicago: University of Chicago Press.

Ball, B. (2000). Getting the facts straight. In T. N. Bethell (Ed.), *Insuring the essentials: Bob Ball on social security* (pp. 247–272). New York: Twentieth Century Foundation Press.

Beattie, R. and McGillvray, W. (1995). A risky strategy: Reflections on the World Bank report "Averting the old age crisis," *International Social Security Review, 48*(1), 5–22.

Blahous, C. P. (2000). *Reforming social security: For ourselves and for our posterity*. Westport, CT: Praeger.

Borzutsky, S. (1991). The Chicago boys, social security and welfare in Chile. In H. Glennerster and J. Midgley (Eds.), *The radical right and the welfare state: An international assessment* (pp. 79–99). Savage, MD: Barnes & Noble.

Borzutsky, S. (1997). Privatizing social security: Relevance of the Chilean experience. In J. Midgley and M. Sherraden (Eds.), *Alternatives to social security: An international inquiry* (pp. 75–90). Westport, CT: Auburn House.

Borzutsky, S. (2001). Chile: Has social security privatization fostered economic development? *International Journal of Social Welfare, 10* 294–299.

Cockburn, C. (1980). The role of social security in development. *International Social Security Review, 33,* 337–358.

Dixon, J. (1982). Provident funds in the third world: A cross-national review. *Public Administration and Development 2*(4), 325–344.

Dixon, J. (1999). *Social security in global perspective.* Westport, CT: Praegar.

Chile: The pension's not-quite miracle. (1998, April 18). *The Economist.*

Edwards, S. (1998). The Chilean pension reform: A pioneering program. In M. Feldstein (Ed.), *Privatizing social security* (pp. 33–62). Chicago: University of Chicago Press.

Evans, M. (1998). Social security: Dismantling the pyramids? In H. Glennerster & J. Hills (Eds.), *The state of welfare: The economics of public spending* (pp. 257–307). Oxford: Oxford University Press.

Feldstein, M. (1974). Social security, induced retirement and aggregate capital accumulation, *Journal of Political Economy 83*(4), 447–475.

Feldstein, M. B. (1977) Social security. In Michael J. Boskin (Ed.), *The crisis in social security: Problems and prospects* (pp. 17–30). San Francisco, CA: Institute for Contemporary Studies.

Feldstein, M. (Ed.). (1998). *Privatizing social security.* Chicago: University of Chicago Press.

Ferrara, P. J. (1982). *Social security: Averting the crisis.* Washington, DC: Cato Institute.

Freeman, R. A. (1981). *The wayward welfare state.* Stanford, CA: Hoover Institution Press.

Glennerster, H. (1995). *British social policy since 1945.* Oxford: Blackwell.

Gillion, C. and Bonilla, A. (1992). An analysis of a national private pension scheme: The case of Chile. *International Labour Review, 131*(3), 171–195.

Graetz, M. J. & Mashaw, J. L. (1999). *True security: Rethinking American social insurance.* New Haven: Yale University Press.

Hewitt, M. (1999). New Labour and social security. In M. Powell (Ed.), *New Labour, new welfare state?* (pp. 149–170). Bristol: Policy Press.

Hills, J., Ditch J. & Glennerster, H. (Eds.) (1994). *Beveridge and social security.* Oxford: Clarendon Press.

International Labour Office (1984). *Introduction to social security.* Geneva: Author.

James, E. (1997). *New systems for old age security: Theory, practice and empirical evidence.* Washington, DC: World Bank.

Kinsgon, E. R. & Williamson, J. B. (1998). Understanding the debate over the privatization of social security. *Journal of Sociology & Social Welfare. 25*(3), 47–62.

Lee Kuan Yew. (2000). *From Third World to first: The Singapore story 1965–2000.* New York: Harper Collins.

Mesa-Lago, C. (1978). *Social security in Latin America.* Pittsburgh: University of Pittsburgh Press.

Mesa-Lago, C. (1994). *Changing social security in Latin America and the Caribbean: Towards alleviating the costs of economic reform.* Boulder, CO: Lynne Rienner.

Midgley, J. (1984) *Social security, inequality and the Third World.* New York: Wiley.

Murray, C. (1984). *Losing ground: American social policy 1950–1980.* New York: Basic Books.

Peterson, P. & Howe, N. (1988). *On borrowed time: How the future of entitlement spending threatens America's future.* San Francisco, CA: Institute of Contemporary Studies.

Peterson, P. (1996). *Will America grow up before it grows old?* New York: Random House.

Privatizing social security: Despite the slump, support is solid. (2001, August 13). *Business Week,* p. 41.

Queisser, M. (1995). Chile and beyond: The second generation pension reforms in Latin America. *International Social Security Review, 48*(1), 23–40.

Bush steers social security to Wall Street. (2001, May 3) *San Francisco Chronicle.*

Sherraden, M. (1997). Provident funds and social protection: The case of Singapore. In J. Midgley and M. Sherraden (Eds.), *Alternatives to social security: An international inquiry* (pp. 33–60). London: Auburn House.

Sherraden, M., Nair, S., Vasoo, S. & Ngiam, T. L. (1995). Social policy based on assets: The impact of Singapore's Central Provident Fund. *Asian Journal of Political Sciences. 3*(2), 112–133.

Skidmore, M. (1999). *Social security and its enemies: The case for America's most efficient insurance program.* Boulder, CO: Westview Press.

Steuerle, C. E. & Bakija, J. M. (1994). *Retooling social security for the 21st century: Right and wrong approaches to reform.* Washington, DC: Urban Institute Press.

Vasoo, S. & Lee, J. (forthcoming). 'Singapore: Social development, housing and the central Provident Fund,' *International Journal of Social Welfare*, 10(4) 276–283.

Walker, A. (1998). Older people. In P. Alcock, A. Erskine & M. May (Eds.), *The student's companion to social policy* (pp. 249–256). Oxford: Blackwell.

Wolfe, M. (1968). Social security and development: The Latin American experience. In Everet M. Kassalow (Ed.), *The role of social security in economic development.* (pp. 155–185). Washington, DC: Department of Health, Education and Welfare.

World Bank. (1994). *Averting the old age crisis: Policies to protect the old and promote growth.* Washington, DC.

CHAPTER FIVE

Welfare, Poverty and Social Services: International Experiences

Neil Gilbert

Over the last decade, it has become almost universally accepted that welfare policies heretofore providing "passive" income supports in times of unemployment and financial duress should be replaced by measures designed to stimulate employment and other responsible behaviors—promoting what the Organization for Economic Cooperation and Development (OECD) terms an "active society"(Kalish, 1991). These measures encompass a wide range of reforms linking cash benefits to work-oriented incentives—a trend commonly referred to as "welfare to workfare" (not always with a positive connotation). Stretching across the political spectrum from Sweden to the United States, the introduction of "active" policies has created new incentives and strong pressures for welfare beneficiaries to find work. This chapter examines the various designs of work-oriented policies with an eye to detecting alternative approaches and what they might have to offer.

From official government documents to scholarly analyses of recent reforms throughout the OECD countries, one continually finds discussion about the importance of "active-work-oriented" measures linked with the need to promote *social inclusion*. Thus, the Norwegian 1992 White Paper recommends that "Social insurance schemes should be designed so as to make the 'Work Approach' the first choice for all affected parties, and to prevent unnecessary exclusion or expulsion of vulnerable groups from the labour market." In the United

Kingdom, the 1998 Green Paper on Welfare Reform identifies social exclusion as one of the three key problems that plagues the existing system. International organizations have also joined in battle against social exclusion. By the late 1990s, championing social inclusion had become a serious objective of the World Bank's mission.

In the 1960s and 1970s policy analysts concerned with welfare programs often focused on the problem of poverty and the need for levels of support that afforded a decent standard of living. There was a burgeoning literature on poverty, its causes, conditions, functions, solutions, and measurements. Today, "poverty" per se is a much less fashionable topic of discourse. In the United States studies of welfare recipients from the 1990s onward tend to focus less on conditions of poverty and levels of support than on the recipients' relationships to the labor market and the dynamics of long-term dependency. In much of Europe, analyses of poverty have been replaced by the broader, more diffuse problem of social exclusion.

The socially excluded are usually poor, but they suffer from more than just a shortage of money, they endure multiple deprivations, the cumulative impact of which leaves them detached from the mainstream of society. Broadly defined, Christoph Badelt (1999) sees the problem as involving exclusion from the labor market, goods and services, security, human rights, and land, particularly in developing countries. Measured more narrowly as the proportion of households located simultaneously in the bottom 20 percent of the national distribution of employment, education, and income, one estimate concludes that 2.7 percent of households in Germany, 3.8 percent in the United States, and 4.4 percent in the Netherlands are socially excluded (Goodin, Headey, Muffels, & Divren, 1999). There are other aspects of social exclusion, which involve lack of participation in community life and insufficient access to social benefits. However it is defined, exclusion from a decent paying job rests at the core of this multidimensional concept, and the shift from welfare to workfare policies is offered as a basic antidote to this problem.

European Experiences

The growing use of work-oriented measures in the public assistance policies of most European welfare states incorporates an increasing emphasis on incentives and sanctions (Eardley, 1996). In Denmark the Social Assistance reform of 1997 marked a significant step in the transition from welfare to workfare. Emphasizing the "activation" of welfare recipients, the Danish scheme requires that all persons receiving social assistance participate in formulating individual action plans, which are designed to improve their job skills and to facilitate gainful employment. Activation entails job placements, training, and educational opportunities. And all recipients under the age of 30 are expected to be activated within their first 13 weeks on welfare. Those who reject a fair offer of activation can have their welfare benefits reduced by up to 20 percent (Torfing, 1997).

After the 1994 elections in the Netherlands, "Work, work, and work again!" was the motto of the the the purple coalition (red social democrats and blue liberals) that formed the new government. True to its words, the purple cabinet's 1996 reform of the Social Assistance Act advanced measures to restrict access to welfare, to alter the level of benefits, and to activate those on the rolls. Thus, persons younger than 21 are no longer eligible for social assistance and recent graduates between ages 21 and 27 who are looking for work (and would not qualify for unemployment insurance because they have no labor history) cannot claim welfare benefits for the first six months of their unemployment. The standard level of benefit has been lowered by 20 percent, at the same time that local agencies have increased discretion to supplement the reduced payments by up to 20 percent based on individual circumstances. This flexibility supports an activating strategy that allows local agencies to incorporate incentives and sanctions into the design of individual reintegration plans. The law prescribes a reduction in benefits for participants who do not comply with these plans. This reform not only reinforced the duty to seek gainful employment for those unemployed; it also extended this obligation to single mothers who are now expected to become active on the labor market when their children reach the age of five (van der Veen & Trommel, 1997).

In France, the *Revenu Minimum d'Insertion* was introduced by Prime Minister Michel Rocard in 1988 as a "veritable revolution in welfare entitlement" (Collins, 1990). Designed to aid the poor, in 1996 this program provided allowances ranging from 2,077 French francs for a single claimant to 5,902 French francs for a couple with three children, amounts which are reduced by income from any other sources. But to receive the cash benefits certain requirements must be met.

According to the law, participants are obliged to sign a contract of rehabilitation worked out with a local committee, which embodies a plan of action and a timetable of specific steps to be taken toward "insertion"—a concept that includes a range of activities. This contract is the linchpin in a reciprocal scheme, designed to unite entitlement to financial aid with the duty to exercise individual responsibility. Allowances are reviewed quarterly and can be withdrawn if recipients fail to discharge their contractual obligations (Barbier & Theret, 2001).

In the early 1990s, versions of workfare were introduced to social assistance schemes in Scandinavia. The Social Services Act of 1991 gave local administrations in Norway authority to institute work requirements as a condition of eligibility for welfare benefits. After Swedish welfare expenditures nearly doubled in the first half of the 1990s, similar reforms were initiated which qualified the long-standing social right to public assistance. Although it was not adopted everywhere, the Uppsala model (named after Sweden's fifth largest municipality) required public assistance applicants to develop individual career plans in consultation with welfare officers and employment counselors and to search actively for work (Hort, 2001).

The Experience of the United States

The most extensive efforts in the welfare to workfare movement were initiated in the United States, culminating with the passage of the Personal Responsibility and Work Opportunity Reconciliation Act of 1996. This act eliminated the Aid to Families with Dependent Children (AFDC) program, creating in its place the Temporary Assistance for Needy Families (TANF) program. Under TANF, states receive a fixed level of federal funding to provide income support to poor families with children. The total federal allocation to all states—$15.3 billion a year, plus a $2 billion contingency fund—was based on the amount states spent on AFDC in 1994. As it turned out, this sum was more than adequate to cover the costs of welfare caseloads into 2003, as these caseloads had already declined by almost 48 percent between 1993 and 1999. Nevertheless, by substituting the TANF block grant for the open-ended funding arrangement under AFDC, Congress effectively eliminated the federally guaranteed entitlement to public assistance. TANF gives the states considerable discretion on the use of these grants to provide cash aid, emergency assistance, child care, job training, education, and job subsidies. States also have wide latitude in designing incentives and sanctions to motivate welfare recipients; in California, for example, benefits are linked to school attendance and in Michigan absent fathers who do not make required child support payments lose their driver's license and other professional licenses. Under TANF, States are required to meet strict timetables with respect to employment. Welfare recipients must be engaged in some kind of work-related activity to continue to receive TANF benefits after their first two years of support. The most stringent federal regulation involves the 60-month limit on assistance, which bars states from providing federally funded cash benefits to families for more than a total of five years during their lifetime. States may exempt up to 20 percent of TANF recipients from the federal five-year limit due to family hardship.

The work-oriented reforms in the United States began as demonstration projects in the early 1990s and concluded with the establishment of TANF. Preliminary results show that these reforms were accompanied by a remarkable and unprecedented decline in the welfare caseload, which plunged by 48 percent from the historic high of 5.1 million families in March 1994 to 2.68 million families in March 1999 (Besharov & Germanis, 2000). Precisely how much of the caseload reduction was due to the pressures of reform and how much to the draw of employment opportunities is hard to untangle. The 1990s were a booming period when the unemployment rate fell to a 30 year low of 4.3 percent. One estimate suggests that between 1993 and 1996 the falling unemployment rate accounted for almost 50 percent of the caseload reduction (Danziger, Moffitt, & Pavetti, 1999). Studies in the later years conclude that from 1996 to 1999 only about 10 to 20 percent of the decline could be attributed to the strong economy (Besharov & Germanis, 2000). But the work-oriented reforms also exerted powerful stimuli toward caseload reduction on at least three fronts. First, incentives and sanctions encouraged unemployed welfare recipients to search for jobs and to accept those offered. On this front, initial findings suggest that the most promising efforts to move recipients from welfare to work involve a mix of strategies which emphasizes intensive job search and quick employment—the "work first" approach—combined with on-the-job training and continued education to upgrade skill (Strawn, 1998). Second, time limits and work requirements discourage new applications for welfare from people who might be able to find employment in times of economic expansion. Finally, stringent demands to pursue training and job search activities coupled with the two-year work rule and 60-month time limit place heavy pressures on the many recipients already engaged in unreported work to exit the welfare rolls. A number of studies have clearly established that a significant proportion of welfare recipients regularly work for pay that is not reported (Edin and Lein, 1997; Edin & Jencks, 1992).

Many of the welfare recipients who left the rolls entered low-paying minimum wage jobs. It is widely believed by welfare advocates that people in these jobs remain poor. Yet, Robert Lerman (1998) shows that when the full range of benefits is taken into account, those who exit welfare to work at the minimum wage have a net income above the poverty level. Examining 12 large states in 1997, Lerman calculated the net income for a family of three based on the minimum wage plus any benefits from TANF or food stamps and the earned income tax credit minus payroll taxes and income taxes. The results demonstrate that in every state welfare recipients who went to work 35 hours a week would have a net income well above the official poverty level ($10,610 for a family of two and $13,330 for a family of three in that year); in five of these states (including California and New York) the family's net income would rise above the poverty level for those who worked only 20 hours a week at the minimum wage.

At the same time that many recipients who left the rolls went to work full-time, a surprising number of mothers seemed to be leaving welfare without taking regular jobs. Besharov and Germanis (2000) conclude that only about 50 to 60 percent of those who left and stayed off welfare appeared to be working regularly. Those who left without going to a job drew on other sources of public support including Social Security, Supplemental Security Income, and food stamps; in Alabama the $329 food stamp allotment for a family of three in 1999 was almost twice as high as the welfare benefit. They could also draw support from pre-existing co-residency arrangements. Before the decline in welfare caseloads, at least 37 percent of welfare mothers lived with other adults.

Trends: Contracts And Incentives

A review of welfare reforms over the last decade reveals several trends in implementation among the OECD countries. One of the most important developments since the 1980s is the increasing emphasis on the duties of social welfare beneficiaries to seek paid employment and of administrative agencies to assist in these efforts. In pursuit of this objective, public assistance schemes have introduced quasi-contractual arrangements (sometimes referred to as activation plans), which are formulated by mutual agreement between clients and administrative officials. These plans specify the clients' obligation and right to participate in education, training, job search, subsidized work, and other activities to improve their chances for paid employment along with the agency's obligation to provide a range of supports and opportunities aimed at facilitating the movement of clients from welfare to work (Van der Veen & Trommel, 1997; Hatland, 1998). This development has altered the way social assistance schemes operate. Administrative procedures for the allocation of benefits have moved away from the impartiality and anonymity of social rights framed by bureaucratic formulas toward the more individualized and discretionary dispensations based on case-by-case management. A corollary of this trend is the heightened differentiation among clients of welfare—such as those ready-to-work, in need of training, and in need of special intervention, leaving "street-level bureaucrats" considerable room for shaping policy through local interpretation (Lipsky, 1980).

The bureaucratic implementation of legislative mandates for individual contracts is not always consistent and rigorous. In France, for example, the legislative requirement for a *contrat d'insertion*, an agreement between claimants and their local authorities (specifying the work-and-training-related activities that would be undertaken by claimants) was a major innovation of the Revenu Minimum d'Insertion (RMI) program. It appears, however, that local officials are not all that keen on drawing-up these contracts. Thus, since the program's inception almost 50 percent of RMI beneficiaries have not signed a *contrat d'insertion* and only 5 to 6 percent have been sanctioned for noncompliance (Barbier & Theret, 2001).

The increased emphasis on the beneficiaries' obligation to work in modern reforms of social assistance policy has been accompanied by the expanded use of financial incentives and sanctions to encourage entry into the labor force. This is not to suggest that the use of incentives in social welfare policy is a new idea, but to recognize that it is an idea which has gained considerable support and momentum in recent times. Incentives and sanctions are generally designed to enhance the financial gain of those who work through adjusting the marginal tax rates on public benefits and offering refundable tax credits, and to impose financial penalties on those who refuse to accept work or to participate in work-related activities. While programs in the United States have probably made the most extensive use of incentives/sanctions to influence work-related behavior, one finds these methods employed to varying degrees in most of the industrialized welfare states.

Policy Questions

The introduction of work-oriented reforms has raised a number of questions, which policymakers are struggling to answer. These questions concern the role of government, the nature of work, how to make work pay, what to do about the hard-to-reach, and how to measure the effects of policy.

What is the appropriate form of state intervention? In formulating work-oriented policies a distinction has been made between neo-statist and neo-liberal strategies. According to Torfing (1997), the neo-statist approach in Denmark puts the "emphasis on activation rather than benefit and wage reductions, on education rather than 'forced labor;' on empowerment rather than control and punishment; and on broad workfare programs rather than programs which target only the unemployed." The neo-liberal approach in this context, which he identifies with the U.S. and the U.K., is represented by a strategy of economic sanctions, limited training, and coercion narrowly targeted on the unemployed.

This distinction, however, draws too sharp a line among differences that are clearly more a matter of degree than kind. Sanctions and coercion are not unknown in neo-statist Denmark, for example, where all recipients of cash assistance who are under 30 must be activated within 13 weeks and anyone who rejects a fair offer of activation (such as work, training, or education) can have their cash assistance cut by up to 20 percent. Similarly, under the Youth Allowance scheme, a form of social assistance for people 18 to 24 years old, young people who decline the offer of a job or training are denied any financial assistance (Eardley, et. al., 1996). In the Netherlands, Keizer (2000) reports that guiding public assistance recipients in their search for jobs includes "both carrots—the delivery of relevant information on jobs and training possibilities—and sticks—the threat of sanctions for those who do not make sufficient efforts." At the same time, the requirement for mandatory employment of welfare recipients in the United States is modified by a 20 percent waiver, for those unable to work. Moreover, the coercive "sticks" of welfare reform in the United States are often combined with supportive services. Findings from ten major studies of welfare-to-work programs in the United States showed that the most successful projects, in terms of the participants' earnings and rates of employment, delivered a mix of supportive services, such as education, training, and child care, along with mandatory work requirements (General Accounting Office, 2000). In the United Kingdom, participants in the New Deal program for young people who do not find unsubsidized jobs after a four month "Gateway" period are offered several options, including subsidized employment for six months, a job with an Environment Task Force, and a course of full-time education or training. More than half of the 42,000 participants enrolled in these options at the end of 1998 were in a full-time course of education or training (Judge, 2001).

What are the meanings of "work" and work-related activities? The different ways that countries have sought to "activate" (sometimes referred to as reintegration or insertion) beneficiaries of public assistance and unemployment programs reveals that definitions of work and work-related activities are neither fixed nor self-evident. When eligibility for social benefits requires participation in work or work-related activities, is voluntary community service a work-related activity? While one can assign vocational education as work-related activity, what about the more general liberal arts education? How should self-employment be viewed, particularly for those such as artists, writers, and street corner musicians whose work often may generate little or no income? Should caring for children, the elderly and infirm relatives qualify as a form of work or active participation, as Scherer (1997) proposes? How long does one count looking for work as a work-related activity?

One of the debates that has emerged regarding the definition of work in the United States concerns the relation between the level of compensation for participating in a program which requires community service in exchange for a grant and the level of compensation received by city employees for performing the same type of service. For example, there are more than 1,400 workfare participants in San Francisco who receive grants for performing work such as janitorial duties in public buildings, sweeping city streets, and cleaning public transit vehicles for grants that amount to less than one-half the hourly wage paid to union employees engaged sometimes side-by-side in similar jobs. Welfare advocates claim that the city is taking advantage of needy applicants forcing them to work at below union scale. City officials claim that the workfare recipients are doing community service in a program designed to teach basic work habits: showing up on time, working in a team, and accepting supervision. The issue, in part, revolves around the length of time a recipient spends in the program. That is, after a year or so on the job one would not expect there is much more to be gained in the way of developing basic work habits.

The debate in California took place within the context of a robust economy with the lowest unemployment rates in more than a decade. Questions about the meaning of "work" and the place of public employment schemes take on even greater weight in societies with high unemployment and future prospects of jobless growth, where the public sector may find itself the employer of last resort. In Italy "socially useful jobs" created by public agencies were supposed to avoid routine activities and place the unemployed in special innovative projects dealing with, for instance, environmental protection and urban renewal. However, in practice, most of those enrolled in the publicly subsidized "socially useful jobs" ended up engaged in routine paper-pushing administrative activities (Fargion, 2001).

How to make work pay? To the extent that various reforms to activate welfare recipients are successful, their very success will result in at least two new problems, which are already emerging. That is, the process of activation is likely to enlarge the ranks of the working poor (or very low-paid workers) at the same time that through the use of restrictive measures it dilutes social protection for the weakest and most disadvantaged members of the community, people who are least competent to work and, perhaps, unable to become independent in the face of modern labor force standards. In regard to the working poor, there are at least two ways to make work pay. The first approach is to require a high minimum wage, which insures a decent standard of living to the lowest paid workers. Some argue that this approach may encourage certain types of existing low-wage jobs to be moved to other countries where labor costs are low and to discourage the development of new business that could not afford to pay a high minimum wage.

The second approach involves ameliorative measures, such as the Working Families Tax Credit recently introduced in the United Kingdom, the Family Tax Credit in New Zealand, and the Earned Income Tax Credit in the U.S. (at a maximum of $3,756 to low-income working families with two or more children), which subsidize workers through tax expenditures. The way the U.S. scheme operates is that the value of the EITC rises by 40 cents for every dollar of income until earnings reach $9,390; it begins to decline only after earnings go above $12,250. The EITC is a refundable credit, so workers with two or more children, who are earning $9,390 to $12,250, and do not benefit from the normal tax deductions available to middle-income citizens, are eligible for the maximum $3,756 refund from the government. In addition to the federal program, which treats all working families the same regardless of local taxes and costs of living, local EITCs can be offered to compensate for variations in taxes and standard of living costs. In the U.S., five states—Massachusetts, New York, Minnesota, Vermont, and Wisconsin—have initiated refundable state EITCs, which are calculated as a percent of the federal credit and range from 10 to 43 percent of the federal EITC. The EITC is an example of federal and state governments mediating between the individual and the market, providing an adequate income to those who work by topping up salary earning with a social transfer. In France the "job bonus" established in 2001 is a recent measure through which low-paid workers are subsidized by the tax authorities. The use of tax expenditures to subsidize low-wage employment is one of the important innovations designed to make work pay.

How to respond to the hard to serve? While measures such as the Job Bonus, Family Tax Credit and EITC can provide a social supplement to make employment pay for workers able to enter the labor force, those left behind pose a greater challenge. When the people most willing and able to work are drawn out of the unemployment and social assistance beneficiary pools, those remaining will embody the hardcore—people who are the most difficult to employ. This sharpening of stratification along cognitive and behavioral lines will require that other policy choices be made. As work-oriented policy reforms create pressures and opportunities for employment, we may expect that an increasing number of clients receiving public assistance and unemployment benefits will move into the paid labor force. Already, in the U.S., welfare policy reforms and a robust economy have contributed to a historic decline in public assistance rolls. An analysis of the National Adult Literacy Survey, which tests an individual's ability to apply math and reading skills to every-day situations, indicates that 35 percent of public assistance recipients score in the lowest of five levels of literacy; people in this category are unable to perform tasks such as locate an intersection on a street map, fill out a government benefits application, and total the costs from an order. (An additional 37 percent of recipients placed in the second lowest category). In a similar vein, findings from the Armed Forces Qualifying Test, which measures the application of math and reading skills in an academic context, show that 33 percent of the welfare recipients had very low basic skills, scoring at or below the 10th percentile. An additional 31 percent also scored quite low, placing between the 10th and 25th percentile (Levenson, Reardon, and Schmidt, 1997).

The question of what to do about the hard-to-reach recipients of public aid is not yet as salient as the issue of how to activate the unemployed in general. Anticipating what will soon become a pressing matter, some have suggested that the prospects for those with extremely low levels of literacy and basic skills are so limited that public efforts should begin by trying to improve the life chances of their children through monitoring the recipient's child rearing practices, offering special educational and social services to the children, providing training to enhance parental functioning of the welfare recipient, and placing teen-age mothers and their children under adult supervision in group homes (Gilbert, 1995; Wilson 1996). Others who emphasize the value of work for this population, even if they could not function well in the normal labor market, would favor the expansion of public employment in protected settings. Finally, there is the option of trying to compensate for deficiencies in basic skills though intense efforts at education and rehabilitation. These various measures, of course, carry different price tags and expectations about individual capacities for change.

Measuring effects. Many experiments are underway using individual contracts, varying service packages, fiscal incentives, and sanctions, particularly in the U.S. where millions of dollars are currently invested in studying the results of these initiatives. The classical experimental research design—random assignment of subjects to intervention and control groups—is the most robust method for assessing the effects of various policy measures. Among European countries there are still strong reservations concerning the use of experimental designs to assess work-oriented policy reforms. Although the experimental design works neatly in laboratory settings, various issues arise when applying this method in field settings. First, random assignment is often difficult to achieve due to ethical reasons that argue against denying a control group services or benefits that would be beneficial, and also because implementation can be distorted by allowing control groups other forms of compensatory treatment and the inability to restrict members of the control group from going elsewhere to receive the intervention services. Differential attrition between control and experimental groups can also contaminate the study design. Finally, randomized experiments cannot control for the systemic impact of the experiment itself. When subjects are aware that an experiment is underway and what the desired effects—having fewer children, finding a job, going to school—are, they may adjust their behavior in response to the changing normative environment, which would confound the experimental-control group comparison. As the increasing use of incentives and sanctions invite evaluative efforts, these and other issues about how to measure the effects of policy are gaining greater attention (Besharov, Germanis, & Rossi, 1997). Ultimately the scientific lessons to be learned about the effects of the various welfare reforms implemented in the advanced industrial countries must be based on solid empirical evidence, which is still lacking in many areas.

Lessons from Abroad

What can the United States learn from experiences in other countries? There are at least two ways in which one can approach this question. The first is to examine welfare reform policies that have been subjected to rigorous social scientific research and shown to be effective. The lessons here tell us what works. But, as noted above, the evidence from abroad regarding the impact of specific policy initiatives is thin. On an aggregate level, if the objective of welfare reform is to reduce the recipient caseload, broad empirical indicators reveal that few, if any, of the OECD countries have achieved the level of success experienced in the the United States over the last decade. At the same time, if the broad objective is to provide economic security and prevent poverty, the aggregate empirical indicators show that the approach taken in the United States is not as effective as that of most of the advanced industrial countries, where higher wages and social welfare benefits have lifted a greater proportion of citizens above the poverty level. In the trade-off between work incentives and poverty prevention, the European countries tend to favor higher levels of social benefits over incentives to work. Thus, there are comparatively fewer low-wage jobs in these countries than in the United States. Over the last decade, the European countries have had higher unemployment rates than the United States, but lower rates of poverty. Whether the approach that provides higher social benefits and accepts more unemployment can continue in the context of increasing global competition remains to be seen. In recent years the OECD countries have tightened access to and duration of social benefits (Gilbert & VanVoorhis, 2001).

A second perspective on the question of what lessons policymakers in the United States might glean from the experiences of other countries, involves not so much learning what works as broadening their purview on the range of available policy choices. For example, the effort to distinguish between neo-statist and neo-liberal approaches to welfare reform makes an important point in sensitizing policymakers to alternatives involving the degree to which work-oriented interventions emphasize what might be termed public investment versus social incentive strategies in relation to both individuals and the market. In regard to individuals, public investment strategies aim to improve chances for employment by enhancing human capital through publicly subsidized education and training programs; in contrast, social incentives focus on creating financial benefits and sanctions—the proverbial carrots and sticks—designed to encourage movement into the labor force at the individual's current level of skill, which exerts no upward pressure on wages. In regard to the market, public investment strategies seek to create new jobs for the unemployed through public works while social incentives rely on tax credits and other benefits and sanctions aimed at encouraging private enterprises to hire welfare recipients.

In the absence of jobs being generated by the market economy, work-related welfare reforms are destined to create tremendous tensions as frustrated job-seekers are demoralized by failure to find work. There are a number of ways to mitigate the strains of work-related reforms in the context of high unemployment and jobless growth. One approach is to spread the work in the private sector. This can be achieved both by reducing the full-time work week to four days, a reform implemented in France and by increasing the level of part-time work as in the Netherlands where part-time employment has climbed from 5 percent to 37 percent of total employment over the last two decades—becoming in the process a " normal" form of gainful activity (Walwei and Werner, 2001). Another method is to increase public sector employment by hiring welfare recipients to perform needed public services. The experience in Italy suggests that when public employment is used to satisfy work requirements, considerable planning and creative effort are needed to design this activity in such a way that it embodies meaningful and productive work.

The lessons of how best to approach the strata of welfare recipients least capable of finding employment in the modern economy remain to be learned. The French emphasis on "insertion," which encompasses a range of community service activities as alternatives to paid employment, suggests one way to mitigate the tension between the skills demanded for gainful employment in market economy and some welfare recipients' limited capacities to develop these skills.

References

Badelt, Christoph (1999.) The role of NPOs in policies to combat social exclusion, Social Protection Discussion Paper No. 9912, The World Bank, Washington D.C.

Barbier, Jean-Claude and Bruno Theret (2001). Welfare-to-work or work-to-welfare: The French case, in Neil Gilbert and Rebecca Van Voorhis eds. *Activating the unemployed: A comparative appraisal of work-oriented policies*. Rutgers: Transaction Pubishers.

Besharov, Douglas and Peter Germanis (2000) Welfare reform—four years later, *The Public Interest* (Summer), pp.17–35.

Besharov, Douglas, Peter Germanis, and Peter Rossi. (1997) *Evaluating welfare reform: A guide for scholars and practitioners*. College Park, Md.: University of Maryland.

Collins, Mary. (1990). A guaranteed minimum income in France," *Social Policy and Administration (42)*, 2.

Danziger, Sheldon, Robert Moffitt and LaDonna Pavetti. (1999). *Is welfare reform working? The impact of economic growth and policy changes: A congressional briefing*. Washington D.C.: Consortium of Social Science Associations.

Eardley, Tony. (1996). From safety nets to spring boards? Social assistance and work incentives in the OECD countries, *Social Policy Review 8*, pp. 265–85.

Eardley, Tony, Jonathan Bradshaw, John Ditch, Ian Gough, and Peter Whiteford. (1996). Social assistance in OECD countries: Synthesis report (Paris: OECD).

Edin, Kathryn and Laura Lein. (1997) Work, welfare, and single mothers' economic survival strategies,*American Sociological Review(62)* 2.

Edin, Kathryn and Christopher Jencks. (1992) "Welfare" in Christopher Jencks. *Rethinking social policy.* Cambridge: Harvard University Press, pp.204–236. 1.

Fargion, Valeria (2001). Creeping workfare policies: The case of Italy, in Neil Gilbert and Rebecca Van Voorhis, eds. *Activating the unemployed: A comparative appraisal of work-oriented policies.* New Brunswick: Transaction Publishers.

General Accounting Office (2000). Welfare reform: State sanction policies and number of families affected. Washington D.C.: Government Printing Office.

Gilbert, Neil. (1995). *Welfare justice: Restoring social equity.* New Haven: Yale University Press.

Gilbert, Neil and Rebecca Van Voorhis, eds. (2001) *Activating the unemployed: A comparative appraisal of work-oriented policies.* New Brunswick: Transaction Publishers.

Goodin, Robert, Bruce Headey, Ruud Muffels, Henk-Jan Divren, (1999) *The real worlds of welfare capitalism,* Cambridge: Cambridge University Press.

Hatland, Askel. (1998) *The changing balance between incentives and economic security in Scandinavian unemployment benefit schemes.* Paper presented at the 2nd International Research Conference on Social Security, Jerusalem, January 25–28.

Hort, Sven, (2001). From a generous to a stingy welfare state? Targeting in the swedish welfare system in the 1990s." In Neil Gilbert ed. *Targeting social benefits: International perspectives and trends.* New Brunswick: Transaction Publishers.

Judge, Ken (2001). Evaluating welfare to work in the United Kingdom. In Neil Gilbert and Rebecca Van Voorhis, eds. *Activating the unemployed: A comparative appraisal of work-oriented policies.* New Brunswick: Transaction Publishers.

Kalish, David. (1991). The active society. *Social Security Journal.* (August), pp. 3–9.

Keizer, Piet (2000). Targeting strategies in the Netherlands: Demand management and cost constraint. In Neil Gilbert, ed. *Targeting social benefits: International perspectives and trends.* New Brunswick: Transaction Publishers.

Levenson, Alec, Elaine Reardon, & Stefanie Schmidt. (1997). Welfare reform and the employment prospects of welfare recipients. *Jobs and Capital* VI:3 (Summer), pp. 36–41.

Lerman, Robert. (1998). *Carrots and sticks: How does the new U.S. income support system encourage single parents to work?* Paper presented at the 2nd International Conference on Social Security, Jerusalem, Israel, January 26, 1998.

Lipsky, Michael (1980). *Street-level bureaucracy.* New York: Russell Sage Foundation.

Scherer, Peter. (1997). Socio-economic change and social policy. in *Family, market, and community.* Paris: OECD.

Strawn, Julie. (1998). *Beyond job search or basic education: Rethinking the role of skills in welfare reform.* Washington, D.C.: Center for Law and Social Policy.

van der Veen, Romke and Willem Trommel (1997). *Managed liberalization of the dutch welfare state.* Paper presented at the SASE Conference on Rethinking the Welfare State, Montreal, July 5–7.

Walwei, Ulrich & Heinz Werner (2001). Employment problems and active labour market policies in industrialized countries. in Dalmer Hoskins, Donate Dobernack, and Christaine Kuptsch, eds., *Social security at the dawn of the 21st century: Topical issues and new approaches.* Rutgers, N.J.: Transaction Publishers.

Wilson, James Q. (1996). Beginning with our children. *Policy Review 76* (March–April).

CHAPTER SIX

Mental Health Lessons from Abroad

Janice Wood Wetzel

"**W**orld mental health is first and foremost a question of economic and political welfare"(Desjarlais et al., 1995, p. 15). This is true despite emerging biological indicators for selected disorders such as schizophrenia, bipolar disorder, and Alzheimer's. In making their case that "mental, behavioral, and social health problems are an increasing part of the health burden on all parts of the globe," the researchers of the landmark *Harvard Study*, published in the groundbreaking book, *World Mental Health*, warn that

> hundreds of millions of women, men, and children suffer from mental illnesses; others experience distress from the consequences of violence, dislocation, poverty, and exploitation. . . Women and children suffer an appalling toll of abuse (Desjarlais et al., 1995, p. 4).

The suffering of those at-risk populations is intrinsically connected with their oppression.

The World Health Organization' definition of mental health is particularly relevant to an international understanding of the dynamics that place people at risk. They point out that mental health is grounded in psychological, physical, social, economic, and spiritual well-being, all of which contribute to a person's quality of life. Mental health is unlikely to be achieved in the absence of a supportive familial, social, educational, and economic context. Freedom from violence, discrimination, and unjust treatment are essential as well (WHO, 2002).

While focusing on the repercussions of social and economic conditions on mental health, Desjarlais and his colleagues remain even-handed, cautioning readers that simply improving social conditions and human rights will not make *all* the difference. Theirs is a *necessary but not sufficient* proviso. Those who are most vulnerable socially and economically are most likely to be at risk of poor mental health, but there is no inoculation that precludes illness among people of means or those who are not subjected to violence. Indeed, the assault on human dignity has no borders. Although the *Harvard Study* focuses on low-income countries in the developing world, the authors note that their findings and conclusions are equally appropriate for the relatively developed world of Western Europe and North America. The promotion of mental health and the prevention of mental illness is a shared challenge, a call to action to individuals and families, to communities, to organizations and governments, both domestic and international. While I will not neglect the importance of psychological interventions, my focus, like Desjarlais and his colleagues, will be on the social and economic conditions that affect the psyche, for it is within that dimension that we can learn most from abroad.

Mental health professionals in the West, particularly in the United States, have been faulted for their emphasis on the psyche, downplaying the etiology of social and economic forces. Meanwhile, Eastern cultures have been guilty of the reverse emphasis, sometimes ignoring mental health concerns, or even denying them altogether. One glaring reason for their denial is due to the fierce stigma associated with the concept, a stigma so powerful that there is no word for mental illness in some cultures, while presenting symptoms are radically altered in others. In Southeast Asian cultures, for example, people who are depressed often present with predominantly somatic, rather than psychological symptoms. In some societies not only is a person who is labeled mentally ill shunned for life, but so is the family, whom they view as the repository of the anathema, generations after he or she has died.

Those societies that do recognize mental illness do not necessarily resolve the dilemma. Too often they view any functioning that deviates from the norms of society as mental illness. Powerless individuals who reject their subservient status are a high-risk population in every culture. It is common for women and minorities throughout the world to be labeled mentally ill for that very reason. Seldom is such defiance considered to be evidence of unusual courage, integrity and strength (Viswanathan & Wetzel, 1993). We can learn from those whom we don't wish to emulate, just as we can from those whom we admire. Hence, nowhere is the importance of *Lessons from Abroad* more relevant than in the mental health field.

If only one side of the psychological/societal equation is addressed, the irony is that those who focus on social conditions are more likely to prevent or ameliorate mental illness, despite their apparent disinterest and denial. It is appropriate in the context of this book to focus on examples of such catalytic social conditions. That in no way negates the importance of the psyche in understanding the ramifications of oppression. It is naive to ignore the disproportionate psychological toll that oppressive conditions foster in individuals. The obvious professional need is for the intentional integration of psychological, social and economic conditions within the context of community programs. Only then will effective prevention and intervention be assured.

Depression Synthesis: the PsychoSocial Spectrum Model

Depression is the world's leading mental health problem.Women are two to three times more likely to be afflicted; their second-class status in all societies is often a contributing factor (Desjarlais, 1995). Domestic and international studies agree that serious depression is not only increasing, but is likely to be experienced at an earlier age in each successive generation (Wetzel, 1994). Rival orthodoxies throughout the world compete for prominence as if human beings could be dissected and compartmentalized into psychological, sociological, biological, or even spiritual fragments, depending on their perspective. It is more useful to respect the rich cache of possibilities for understanding human behavior that can provide insight into the mystery of depression. Careful investigation reveals that there are many more commonalities among theories than there are differences.

A detailed analysis of the major theories of depression that are advanced in the Eastern and Western hemispheres reveal four common themes that I have termed Aloneness, Connectedness, Action, and Perception. They are dimensions of human development which together form a *PsychoSocial Spectrum*, a model that provides an easily understood blueprint for prevention and intervention, whatever the culture. Each has a positive dimension reflecting psychological and social catalysts for mental health, and a negative dimension that sets up parallel barriers to mental health, making one vulnerable to depression. By assessing a person's psychosocial condition according to these four developmental lines, appropriate interventions can be created within community programs to enhance mental health, personal growth, and healing. The *PsychoSocial Spectrum*, depicted below in Figure 1, is discussed at length elsewhere in varying contexts (Wetzel, 1991a; 1991b; 1992; 1993).

East versus West Revisited

While the exploration of theoretical approaches brings these common dimensions to light, careful analysis also reveals blatant dichotomies among them. Even the objectives of prevention and intervention, as articulated in Western as contrasted with Eastern philosophies, appear to stand in diametric opposition. For instance, is a fragile ego to blame for depression, as suggested by Western psychoanalytic theories, or is it owing to the inability to relinquish the ego, an Eastern ideal? Is control over one's life, a Western notion, essential to mental health, or must one be unconcerned with personal power as Eastern philosophies instruct us? Must we be oriented toward reaching goals (Western), or is it the process that counts (Eastern)? Are we alone in the world (Western), or are we at-one with it (Eastern)? Should we work toward change (Western), or toward acceptance (Eastern)?

The PsychoSocial Spectrum

	Negative Valence ⟶	Positive Valence
CONNECTEDNESS	Dependent/Living through others ⟶	Relational/Healthy attachments
ALONENESS	Alienated/Lonely ⟶	Independent/Unique
ACTION	Destructive/Fragmented energy ⟶	Constructive/Focused energy
PERCEPTION	Worthlessness/Powerlessness ⟶	Self-esteem/Hopefulness

FIGURE I

Should we strive toward being the best that we can be (Western), or should we accept ourselves as we are (Eastern)? And finally, should we learn to be independent as we are taught in the West, or to be interdependent as the East so wisely counsels? As the list lengthens, it becomes clear that we must accept a both/and dualistic approach to life's paradoxes. Not only should we learn from abroad, but we too have something universal to offer, if one is careful to transfer our knowledge appropriately, while integrating another culture's developmental strengths and challenges. A *PsychoSocial Spectrum* model can provide an encompassing framework for multilevel insight and intervention that respects each philosophical stance within the context of human development and human rights.

Posttraumatic Stress Disorder (PTSD) and Community Violence

Violence in one way or another permeates the lives of people the world over. Mental health is jeopardized, as is physical health. On a large scale, violence comes in the form of wars, torture, and other forms of state repression that leads to civil unrest. Discrimination foments the furor. The collective repercussions on society are not fully understood, although they can be extrapolated from what we have learned about individual and familial violence. Many communities have responded to violence through innovative programs. The Guatemalan Mayan people, for example, have developed a community-based program for children who are psychologically scarred by wartime trauma, emphasizing self-esteem enhancement. It would appear to be a rather bland response were it not for the fact that violence corrodes the very core of one's sense of self-worth. Other programs, such as public responses to ethnic violence in India and Sri Lanka, are institutionally based. There, the police took a central role in averting ethnic riots by taking a firm public stand against such behavior. Politicians followed suit, making it clear that there would be no tolerance for any level of violence or acts of revenge. Desjarlais et al. (1995), in reporting these interventions, make a case for more research to determine general principles to guide public policy and public health interventions based upon comparative studies.

We know from existing public health and World Health Organization statistics, however, that it is women and children who are 79 percent more likely to be victims in wartime than are men in combat (Beijing Platform for Action, 1995). We must apply to these civilian survivors, as well as to combatants, what we have learned about post-traumatic stress disorder (PTSD), the fifth most diagnosed psychiatric disorder in the United States. An estimated 5 percent of Americans, more than 13 million people, have PTSD at any given time, yet fewer than 30 percent of those who have the symptoms seek treatment for their condition. Symptoms include nightmares, loss of appetite, sadness, fear, confusion, and isolation.

International research confirms that once diagnosed, PTSD is treatable with psychotherapy, medication, or a combination of both (International Society for Posttraumatic Stress Studies, 1998). Treatment may help people recover even if initiated in the years following the trauma and the onset of symptoms. Tragically, in many cases, the causes and symptoms of PTSD are not widely understood. Because of this, the problem can be misdiagnosed and often is not even considered as a possible diagnosis. This lack of understanding and awareness can exact a devastating personal toll for years to come on a person with PTSD and those who are close to him or her.

PTSD often affects combat victims, survivors of serious accidents, natural disasters, or other major catastrophic events, such as plane crashes or terrorist attacks. Also affected are survivors of interpersonal violence such as physical or sexual assault, including childhood abuse and violence against women and the elderly.

In a statement on Social and Human Rights Questions to the United Nations' Economic and Social Council in July of 1998, the International Society for Posttraumatic Stress Studies observed that "'loud' emergency situations, such as armed conflict, draw the attention of the international community, while the 'silent' emergencies, such as poverty, famine and homelessness—which claim more victims each year—are largely forgotten." They also noted that "not enough attention is given to the provision of services for traumatized help-givers." We can certainly bring that knowledge home and apply it to good advantage.

Community Trauma and Psychodrama

In 1942, an Italian psychiatrist, J.L. Moreno, brought psychodrama to the West as a therapeutic method that allows people to dramatize in a group setting that which they otherwise only talk about individually. Over the years, Moreno's psychodrama lost its cache in most Western helping professions. Paradoxically, it has become one of the leading international interventions for people who are trying to come to terms with the trauma spawned by the disintegration of their societies. Torture, rape, murder of loved ones, looting and burning of their homes and their land are typical of the atrocities experienced by the survivors at the hands of people they knew so well. This is as true in Croatia, Bosnia, and Kosovo as it is in Rwanda. Their mental health problems have skyrocketed, challenging the healing professions with the overwhelming question, "How can people pick up the pieces of their lives after having lived through the inhumanity inflicted by former friends and neighbors" (Z. Bolton, personal communication, November 22, 2000)? In answering the question, psychodrama and its worldwide followers are bridging the psychological and social divide to unparalleled effect. At international conferences, psychodrama therapists from many disciplines confer in language-specific groups such as Hebrew, Japanese, Korean, French, Italian, Spanish, Portuguese and English, to share their experience, insights and challenging professional issues.

As psychodrama is played out, the facilitator is in the role of director, the client is usually the protagonist, while others take the part of designated auxiliary egos and the audience. Verbal and nonverbal role plays and dramatizations are utilized in the process of playing out dreams and life events, altering them to psychological advantage (Blatner, 2000). Techniques include role reversal, doubling, mirroring, concretizing, maximizing, and soliloquy (Kellerman, 1992). Thus, the insights of ego-psychology, cognitive-behavioral principles, narrative axioms, and group dynamics are all brought to bear on the psyche in the aftermath of horrendous life events. The key to the model, however, is not just in the revisiting the experience on the therapeutic stage, but being afforded the gift of rewriting their psychological script and in so doing, healing and persevering.

The Battering of Women

Not unrelated is violence against women, a cross-cutting issue that assaults not only their bodies but their minds. It takes many forms . . . as the spoils of war, sexual and reproductive domination and control by men, and the universal demand for female subservience in male/female relationships within and outside the home. The battering of women by men in their lives is a worldwide atrocity. Such women are four to five times more likely to require mental health treatment and five times more likely to attempt suicide than non-battered women (Warren, 1991). What is more, there is evidence that major depression, anxiety, alcohol and drug dependency, as well as eating disorders are also linked to a history of female abuse, both sexual and otherwise physical (Wetzel, 1995, 2000; Desjarlais et al., 1995).

The international Violence Against Women (domestic violence) community is fraught with controversy. While many services have been aware of attending to PTSD, depression, and anxiety in tandem with finding haven in safe houses, the resultant retribution from perpetrators (the men in their lives) has often been lethal when women leave home. Research and expert experience have shown that a woman's risk to her life, not to mention further brutalizing, is most serious when she leaves her batterer. The conundrum is that she is at risk if she stays, and at even greater risk if she leaves. While there has been no resolution to the troubling dilemma, lessons from abroad can provide insights through their experiences.

Queensland Health in Australia argues for the need to explore how women can be safe at home, given the fact that only a small percentage of at-risk women in the past have indicated an interest in accessing services, based in part on understandable fear. Such women are already traumatized and have internalized the spoken and unspoken demeaning messages about their subservient, worthless status as females. To expect them to face yet another life-threatening hurdle may be more than they can bear. Queensland Health has found that stigma plays a role in their reticence as well. They report that once women understand that the battering is not their fault, they are more likely to choose to find refuge in shelters. Their increasing numbers supports this premise. In Australia, while pioneer responses to violence twenty years ago were based on women's shelters, today there are other options, in part developed by women who resided and later worked in them. The growth of counseling, group advocacy, and education services are based on the knowledge and experiences of such women, having identified how and what could and, in their opinions, must be done better to enable them to be free of male violence in relationships. Attention to the batterer is one example.

Attention to Male Batterers

There has been recognition in the domestic violence sector, for at least 10 years now, about the injustice of women and children having to leave their homes, while the offender continues to live at home. It is primarily through the lobbying and advocacy work of women's shelters and domestic violence services that provision such as "ouster orders" to enable the removal of the offender from the family home has been archived in the Queensland domestic violence legislation. However, while the spirit of the legislation is commendable, the application and enforcement issues still make the full realization of this provision a vexing one, and cannot guarantee the safety of women and children in a location where the offender has easy access to them. The bottom-line issue remains the civil response to a crime, which leads to inadequate outcomes for women and children. In many cases, safety issues force them to leave their family home. Women's shelters and other domestic violence services have been instrumental in fostering governmental support to formalize the criminality of domestic violence (Stratigos, 2000).

Thanks to women's advocacy groups, there has been an unprecedented increase in the number of women and children seeking safety in women's shelters in Queensland. Their success has spawned a shelter space problem in recent years, making it necessary for more and more women to be placed in alternative accommodations such as motels. Advocates underscore the importance of keeping domestic violence on the public agenda, working diligently to maintain it there. The challenge to resistant legislators and courts is in fact universal. The role of community-based services is systemic and structural as well, calling for advocacy beyond the typical service delivery model. If women and children are to lead violence-free lives, it is important that all sectors (including government) work together to raise the quality and quantity of response to domestic violence, acknowledging the need for a diversity of responses and their development (Stratigos, 2000).

In Canada, the government has created optional shelters for men who batter, in lieu of prisons. Ostensibly rehabilitative, the truth is that instead of focusing on their damaging attitudes and behavior toward women, the offenders spend their time developing men's support groups to strengthen demands to their right to child custody, and to reinforce the traditional values that they believe are their intrinsic right as heads of families. Martin Dufresne (2000), a women's advocate in Canada, concludes that doing so is a "cruel joke," given that the problem of ensuring women's safety either at home or in shelters has emerged due to the reluctance of society to effectively keep women safe from their abusers.

In 1998, Israel took a similar route, but with safeguards, when it created a house for men who batter. They call it NOAM, meaning gentleness. The men enter freely, not under court order, and go to work each day, sharing responsibilities for chores, and so on, much as a commune might. The program emphasizes the re-learning of social skills and holds group therapy sessions each evening. Even though they have had a successful track record, female domestic violence workers do not feel that male rehabilitation homes are the solution to Israel's epidemic of violence against women. They are concerned that NOAM receives much public attention from the media because there are very few intervention programs in the country. In fact, court ordered rehabilitation is non-existent. Israel has an estimated 200,000 male batterers, and hundreds of convictions each year. NOAM, with 20–30 men at any given time and a budget of $250,000, is a very costly way of rehabilitating those batterers. The Haifa Women's Coalition points out that feminist women set up almost all hotlines and facilities for female victims of domestic violence and rape. It is questionable that men would develop male rehabilitation services for the perpetrators. Since the state still thinks domestic violence is a women's problem, the state is unlikely to do so. The women in the coalition doubt that the majority of men who are violent to their partners would choose to live in a shelter and undergo group therapy of their own free will. If it were ordered by the courts, would there be the same success rates? The question remains unless we answer these lessons from abroad.

The Haifa Women's Coalition already know they must resist governmental insistence on pitting women's shelters against one another, while reducing funds to supplement them. At the time of this writing, a case is presently before the Israel Supreme Court to counter the government's efforts to close down the present management of the only existing Palestinian-Israeli shelter for women, and to allow any one of the other six vying Jewish women's groups, or any other organization for that matter, to run it (Paula Mills, 2000). Such forced competition for resources is a matter of course in the United States.

The resolve of the women of Haifa, in my opinion, is exemplary and should be considered as a model of advocacy.

Refugees and Rape

Rape is a common experience associated with refugee women and girls of all ages. As in other venues, it is not primarily a sexual act, but a way for men to gain control and to exhibit power. The World Health Organization (WHO), in collaboration with the Office of the United Nations High Commissioner for Refugees (UNHCR), reports that refugee females are at risk of being raped in their countries of origin, during passage, in resettlement camps, and in the country where they finally settle (1996). The perpetrators are generally the very men who are supposed to protect them: border guards, patrolmen, other refugees, husbands and male relatives, as well as pirates on the seas, and "cayottes" who are paid large sums to help refugees flee their countries illegally. In developing countries, the chastity of women often is wedded to the notion of family honor, so if she is raped, she is blamed for the rape itself and shunned or violently punished without recourse. Raped women are considered unclean and less valuable, and so are discouraged from revealing the rape. Thus, the physical and psychological trauma of rape is compounded. Unable to trust those closest to them who are also the most powerful people in their lives, without societal support or recourse for their victimization, they obviously would be vulnerable to emotional distress. To imagine otherwise is to dismiss their humanity.

The UNHCR recommendations are made for refugees in camps, but they are just as pertinent to survivors who reach our shores. They suggest that refugee counselors look for signs of PTSD and physical violence that may be the result of the assault, or retaliation from family members after the fact. They should be encouraged to speak privately with a female counselor. The victims should be taught some ways that they might avoid being raped again. Support groups are useful, therapeutically as well as for protection. It is also suggested that women be encouraged to become active in the women's community to facilitate recovery from emotional and social scars. Healing is fostered through individual understanding and mutual support, and by means of collective action on behalf of women. Perhaps inadvertently, the UNHCR endorses feminist teachings. The bottom line is that women should be provided mutual support and the opportunity for collective social action in order to change social conditions that spawn sexual violence. Because the social oppression of women is at the core of their vulnerability to rape and its psychological repercussions, targeting their oppression as an intervention is a preventive tactic.

The psychology of rape and its hidden aspects also may be perpetrated on men and boys, although this is not as common an occurrence. They, too, keep the secret, but for different reasons. They feel it is too difficult to admit to because of the association of rape with females and their perception of weakness. Thus, they too should be encouraged to speak with a counselor privately, preferably a male. Refugee workers believe it best to couple same-sex counselors with female and male victims so that they may talk more freely. As with females, it is advised to look for symptoms of PTSD. In all cases, strict confidentiality is so essential that the chance of false perceptions must be guarded. Efforts should be made not to repeat similar stories publically that the refugee might consider personal, even if they are not. It is important, too, not to make the victim repeat her or his story over and over. Find ways of ending their social isolation, let them know they are not alone in their experience, and that the rape is not their fault. The expression of anger at the rapist is to be encouraged within the safety of the counseling relationship.

The WHO and UNHCR also suggest that relief workers and people providing services should organize to discuss the problems of rape victims and improvement of services. Religious leaders also should be made aware of the importance of the healing process for both victims and their families. They can do a great deal to help them, in part by educating men to be compassionate, and helping them to change their attitudes toward women. Meetings in the community should be held by religious and community leaders, perhaps offering special prayers as part of the healing process. In sum, community participation is key at all phases and levels of service provision from planning and policy development to personal counseling and group and community programs.

Refugees are often difficult to engage because of the trauma they have undergone, culture shock, fear of being deported or detained, and privacy issues pertinent to their ethnic and religious customs. Social workers who have years of expertise working with refugees from all over the world find that even the most inhibited can be reached when the interviewer relieves their anxieties and shows sincere interest in them. They do so by beginning with the simple, open-ended questions, "Would you tell me about your country, where you grew up and went to school?" Then, "Tell me about your journey to America. What was it like?" Or the open-ended question, "Tell me your story. How did you get here? What happened?" (Shamitz, 1997).

Poverty and Mental Health

According to the United Nations, poverty is the ultimate violence (UN, 1995). Poverty has proven to be another cross-cutting issue inexorably linked to mental illness vulnerability (Desjarlais, 1995). Women again are the population at risk the world over. According to the UN, women do two thirds of the world's work, yet two thirds of all women in the world live in poverty. The largest poverty population is female headed households that are estimated to represent one third of all households in the world. In the U.S., 78 percent of all people living in poverty are single women and their children. And the second largest poverty group in the world and in the U.S. are the elderly, approximately 79 percent of whom are women. Together, single young and elderly women make up over 70 percent of the poor in most countries. In the U.S., homelessness is a way of life for an estimated 2 million citizens each year, with single women and their 700,000 children the fastest growing segment of the homeless population. Single women represent 10 to 14 percent of the total number of homeless. Rather than blaming them for their condition, they should be acknowledged for having taken responsibility for their children and families. It is society that insists on dismissing their care-taking work within and outside of the home, depriving them of life-sustaining wages or any wages at all, and denying them affordable child care and reasonable housing. They are criticized for child neglect if they work outside the home and faulted if they don't. Such double binds are spoken of as examples of women's oppression. They are also called "crazy-making" (Wetzel, 1993; Frye, 1995).

It is not just the double-bind situation that affects women's mental health. It is the devastating link between poverty and the mistreatment of girls and women throughout the world. Van Wormer (1997) makes their physical and mental plight as clear as it is tragic:

Where survival is at stake, daughters are sacrificed for sons. Girls may be sold to brothels for the highest bidder. In Thailand, for example, whole villages are being depleted by the deaths of daughters sold into slave-prostitution who then return home to die along with their HIV-infected babies. In sub-Saharan Africa, one adult in forty is HIV-infected [as a result of women's subservient condition]. In India, poverty breeds dowry burnings of brides whose families are unable to meet dowry obligations (pp. 265–266).

She goes on to say, "Just as we dehumanize the enemy during wartime in order to reduce any qualms in battle, so we dehumanize the poor and homeless in order to justify our handling of them (van Wormer, 1997, p. 266). What could be more detrimental to mental health than dehumanization?

Although urban poverty is growing, rural poverty still accounts for over 80 percent of the world's poor, resulting in chronic hunger and malnutrition that predictably affects the biochemistry of its victims, and in turn bodily and psychological distress. But contrary to conventional wisdom, as Desjarlais et al. (1995) point out, mental disorders appear to increase when living conditions are improving. Although they stress the importance of advocating for better conditions for people living in poverty, given their high-risk status, they conclude that economics alone is not the answer to psychological well-being. The Italian political philosopher and statesman, Machiavelli (1532/1984), noted the phenomenon. In *The Prince*, his renowned amoral book on how to exert power, he suggested that there is more unrest among those who are oppressed when their prospects become more likely and hope is on the horizon. When they feel totally bereft, without perceived possibility, they are less likely to rebel. His recommendation to those who would wish to maintain power, then, was a foregone conclusion. Elizabeth Cady Stanton and her suffragist colleagues put it similarly when they declared, "Women's discontent increases in exact proportion to her development" (1985/1881). Their observation was in no way meant to deter women from reaching their potential.

The divergent conclusions based upon the same observations only bring home the fact that knowledge can be used to the advantage or disadvantage of those who are subjugated and thus at risk. It is the social worker's job to be sure that knowledge is used constructively, not abusively. A case in point: While nations acknowledge the high-risk status of women in poverty, they universally blame them for their plight, rather than addressing the root causes. The United States is no exception, clearly reflected in the welfare policies that demand that they work outside the home to support their families although there are few jobs with life-sustaining wages available to them. This is an example of "responsibility without possibility," an aspect of the "crazy-making" alluded to earlier. Social and economic development is a major antidote to the problems of the poor, whether female or male. By extension, it is also an antidote to their mental health risk.

Social and Economic Development

In assessing international social and economic development in the 20th century, UNICEF (1989) presented what they called "seven sins" of development from which the difference between success and failure can be understood. They remain viable measures in their own right, but when we recognize the intrinsic importance of social development to mental health, they take on even greater importance. *Development without the Poor*, according to UNICEF, is one of the "sins." They contend, in fact, that the greatest challenge of social development is the challenge of meeting the needs of the very poorest people. UNICEF notes that development in the developing world has historically been confined to showcase examples and pilot projects, and fails to reach the vast majority of the poor, which happens in more developed countries as well. There must be a shift towards applying the knowledge that we have on a scale commensurate with the need. The reasons for failing to do so are complex. Among them are the lack of pressure to sustain efforts, representation of the poor in decision-making, and the inversion of spending pyramids, so that the majority of resources available for development are not devoted to action that benefits the poorest. Given that women are disproportionately represented among the poor, their absence takes its toll on them, and on social development efforts that have been shown to fail when women are ignored. The result is their increased vulnerability to emotional distress in direct proportion to their social and economic oppression.

UNICEF also makes two other points relevant to mental health and poverty. *Development without the Achievable* points to the importance of clearly addressing priorities or step-by-step implementation directives so that others can apply the knowledge. Many well-formed plans remain on the shelf, they argue, not due to political will alone, but to the lack of this kind of hands-on information. Knowledge for the 21st century must be shaped into plans capable of attracting whatever political will is available, while using persuasive means to increase it. The challenge, given the fierce competition for resources, is the molding of available knowledge into achievable, large scale, low cost, high impact, and politically attractive plans. To my mind, the call to social work is loud and clear if the profession wants to be effective in the mental health service arena.

Speaking of *Development without Mobilization* as the seventh "sin," UNICEF challenges us to put contemporary knowledge at the disposal of the majority. The dissemination of essential development knowledge, particularly regarding health, has been left out of health services which have had neither the time, training, nor outreach mechanisms to do the job. The same can be said of mental health, an aspect of health too often overlooked even by UNICEF. There now is an unprecedented capacity to communicate state-of-the-art knowledge around the world. School systems, radio, and television are likely media. Even the computer is becoming ubiquitous in many communities today, particularly in local libraries and other public gathering places. Mental health will be greatly enhanced in the process of closing the so-called "digital divide." Tens of thousands of nongovernmental organizations, including women's programs, are working in the poorest communities. By mobilizing social capacities of the people, the major threats to life and health can be alleviated (Wetzel, 1993).

Probably the world's most successful economic development program is the Grameen Bank of Dhaka, Bangladesh, founded in 1976 by Muhammad Yunus, an economist who was making loans for commercial banks. (Grameen means "rural" or "village" in English.) Yunus was appalled by the living conditions of people in rural Bangladesh, the second poorest nation in the world. He was struck especially by the severe situation of women who are in a particularly precarious position when they are abandoned or divorced. They have no means of livelihood, and their families will not allow them to return to their homes. Consequently, the self-esteem of these women is as impoverished as their economic wherewithal. Banks would not grant them loans without collateral guarantees, so Yunus decided to become a personal benefactor to the region for micro-enterprises for low-income women. His credit union was opened to men as well, but 77 percent of the loans continue to be granted to women. Their payback rate has proven to be even better than their male counterparts. Because people without wherewithal seldom have access to credit, the Grameen model requires the group members themselves to become the collateral, promising to pay any outstanding debt that is not paid by the grantee. It has seldom been necessary to do so (Yunus & Jolis, 1999).

A follow-up study a few years ago showed that one third of the Grameen borrowers had escaped poverty. The model has proven to be so successful that the program has spread not only all throughout the developing world, but to low-income areas of the developed world as well. Today, more than eight million people in more than 58 countries receive micro-credit loans (Rosenberg, 2000). While I was interviewing the officers of the Grameen Bank in Dhaka, urban planners in Chicago and Denver happened to call, requesting the details of the Grameen model to be applied in their inner cities. The World Bank itself has been influenced to such an extent that it has developed a micro-credit program for people in poverty. It has acknowledged the success of the program and its importance to the development of poor communities, as well as the necessity of focusing on women, for their own sake, and for the sake of their communities.

The success of the model is based on more than a traditional banking enterprise. It focuses on self-esteem and personal development (more culturally palatable terms than mental health and mental illness), as well as the importance of group support and collaboration in reaching their goals. These components are considered to be key to the success of the Grameen model. Banking becomes an unusual method of achieving human rights and dignity, without losing sight of the philosophy that the poor should receive what is rightly theirs already. Again, the World Bank has been moved to follow suit, having developed a mental health division within the organization itself. In my opinion, this synthesis of psychological, social, and economic development should be considered a crucial lesson for development, absolutely critical to the fulfillment of human rights which is, after all, the ultimate objective.

Whether or not the World Bank incorporates Grameen's *Train the Trainers* economic development programs that they conduct for landless women and children is yet to be seen. The *Train the Trainers* model is common in women's communities of the developing world, and to my mind is a natural model for social workers everywhere.

Women who show skill at leadership create centers in their villages in which to teach other women. The training includes knowledge about child survival, communications, and networking so that women can involve others in their communities in the principles of unity and discipline that they have learned. There is even evidence that their sons and daughters are changing their negative perspectives about girls and women, ending the subservient condition of females in the next generation (Quanine, 1989; Wetzel, 1993). This long-term vision is key to societal change in the interest of the poor.

Hernando de Soto of Peru, also an economist, has had another intriguing idea, if more difficult to implement (Rosenberg, 2000). He argues that the precarious houses and makeshift enterprises that are symbols of poverty throughout the world are also assets deserving of credit. From his perspective, the world's poor own trillions of dollars worth of assets. They cannot access credit only because they don't hold title to their houses, businesses, and farms like the middle class does; their holdings are said to be informal. Therefore, they cannot use them as collateral for loans, sell stakes in their businesses, or buy insurance to minimize risk. De Soto posits that the reason that capitalism triumphs in the West and fails in less developed countries lies not in political culture, geography, or work ethic. Rather, it is because of the mundane world of property registries. The poor, he argues, would become successful if they were granted the same property titles as others have. He is hoping to foment an economic revolution, joining with the microcredit revolution already underway. His first property registry was in Peru where 1.3 million buildings and 300,000 businesses were titled from 1991–1994. Now he and his team are doing similar work in other countries (Rosenberg, 2000). We can learn from de Soto, as we can from Yunus, but the message goes beyond their particular models. Their genius stems from the fact that they have taken a fresh look at a situation that appears to be intractable, not only making a difference by enhancing the quality of life for thousands of people, but by engendering self-esteem, dignity, and human rights in the process. Theirs is indeed a mental health lesson from abroad worth noting.

Mental Health and the Workplace

"According to the International Labour Organisation (ILO), mental illness [affects] more human lives and gives rise to a greater waste of human resources than all other forms of disability" (Harnois & Gabriel, 2000, p. 19). The Mental Health Policy and Development Department of Mental Health and Substance Dependence, Noncommunicable Diseases and Mental Health, divisions of the World Health Organization, and the International Labour Organisation (ILO) have reported on the subject of mental health and work throughout the world, providing examples of problems, accomplishments and their impact on afflicted people.

The employment rate of the mentally challenged is about 90 percent. To put it another way, only about 10 percent of people with serious mental health problems who wish to work are judged capable of doing so (Harnois & Gabriel, 2000). "Women," the ILO notes, "fare less well than men" (p. 19). It is not surprising that depression is by far the most common diagnosis. The gender difference seems to be consistent with other areas of vulnerability that are also linked. The inability to earn a living can lead to impoverishment, which in turn may worsen the illness. Given the already high rates of poverty among women, finding stable means of support and productivity is important to their sense of self-esteem and quality of life, and in turn to improving their at-risk status for mental illness.

The challenges associated with mental illness and the workplace are being addressed worldwide. While the United States can take pride in its efforts to address these problems through the American Rehabilitation Act, there are many programs from abroad that the World Health Organization speaks of as "good practices" from which we can learn. For example, in Beijing, China, one of the country's largest cotton factories has several hundred apartments, a 140-bed hospital, and two schools, all the responsibility of the employer. Accommodation for a schizophrenic woman who was hospitalized for two years was said to be typical. She was visited in the hospital on a regular basis by her manager and fellow factory workers. When she returned to her job on the "cotton chain" the employer gave her full pay, and within a month she was as productive as her co-workers on the assembly line. She was able to function alone in her apartment as well.

In a number of countries in Europe, *social firms* are being developed which are medium-sized enterprises for the primary purpose of providing employment for people with mental disabilities in a context which is similar to a regular firm, but which provides the required support that they need. The mentally ill work side by side with non-disabled people and are paid regular wages on the basis of a regular work contract. They all have the same rights and obligations. The EU has been singled out as having provided exemplary support for the development and evaluation of social firms that have fostered transnational cooperation. Participating countries have been able to exchange views, experiences, problems and solutions. When Italian cooperatives are included in the count, there are thought to be more than 2000 social firms in Europe today, all of which offer employment and support to people with psychiatric disabilities. Their mission is both social and commercial. The atmosphere, as compared with regular businesses, is designed to be empowering and welcoming. The emphasis in the social firm is on the abilities and potential of the worker, rather than on the potential barriers and problems. Their flexible approach often results in jobs being accomplished just as quickly as in any other workplace, and to just as high a standard.

Italy has been known for its avant garde mental health legislation ever since 1978, when it stopped admissions to psychiatric hospitals as well as prescribed treatment in community mental health centers, allowing hospitalizations only in general hospitals with fewer than 15 beds. *Social cooperatives* were set up which function independently of mental health services, but maintain a close working relationship with them. Many cooperatives share the "social firm philosophy" that espouses finding a place in the labor market, with a protected workplace for the mentally impaired. In 1991, an Italian law established two types of social cooperatives. One type aims to provide social and health assistance where the workers are involved in the management of care centers, many providing rehabilitation packages and professional education programs. Another type aims to promote job opportunities for people with disabilities. Both must employ a minimum of 30 percent of people with disabilities if they are to receive government grants. More than 700 social cooperatives exist in Italy today.

Another best practices program is a major nongovernmental organization (NGO) in Spain which has created 12 service centers employing more than 800 mentally ill people who fill 183 service contracts for a modern commercial furniture factory. The vast majority of participants have had long stays in psychiatric hospitals. When they are working, they live nearby, many enjoying a residential swimming pool on the premises. They are well accepted in the community due in part to the ongoing collaboration between the city council and the "workshop" leaders. An on-site research center is affiliated with the University of Cordoba which focuses on rehabilitation research. The cooperative is 90 percent self-financed, but like all of the European programs reported, it receives funding within the auspices of two EU programs, Horizon and Helios 1 and 2.

In sum, WHO and the ILO (2000) have concluded that "the workplace is one of the key environments that affect our mental well-being and health" (2000, p. 8). Employment, in fact, provides five categories of psychological experience they believe promote mental well-being. They are: 1) the importance of time structure to psychological health; 2) the provision of social contact; 3) collective effort and purpose that offer a social context other than the family; 4) social identity based upon the fact that employment provides an important element in defining oneself; and 5) regular activity that serves to organize one's daily life. Taking the time to include employees in planning and implementing activities and events in the workplace pays untold dividends because it promotes psychological well-being and mental health without cost to the employer.

The Internet as an International Resource

The Internet is proving to be a useful global resource for people who are suffering from mental illnesses. Whatever the diagnosis, there are international networks that provide information, referrals, and opportunities to discuss their problems with peers and professionals. Schizophrenia, the most disabling of the major mental illnesses, is just one example. Most recently, the World Fellowship for Schizophrenia and Allied Disorders (www.world-schizophrenia.org) published international conference proceedings on the web, an article on the important contribution of families in the rehabilitation of loved ones, aspects of social stigma, recommended books, and the organization's board members and personnel. Another international website, Schizophrenics Anonymous (www.sanonymous.org) is a confidential self-help support network available in Spanish, French, German, and English that purports 1) to help restore dignity and sense of purpose for persons who are working for recovery from schizophrenia or related disorders; 2) to offer fellowship, positive support, and companionship in order to achieve good mental health; 3) to improve schizophrencis' own attitudes about their lives and illness; 4) to provide members with the latest information regarding schizophrenia; and 5) to encourage members to take positive steps towards recovery from the illness (p. 3). Self-help programs of this nature are a boon to the mentally ill, to their families, and to professionals who can augment their interventions with these contemporary "tools" unknown to generations of yesteryear.

Conclusion

The transference of mental health lessons from abroad to the people of the United States is not only appropriate, it is essential in this era of diminishing resources and reduced services. Community prevention of mental illness and promotion of mental health in the context of social and economic development is fundamental to countering unmet escalating intrapsychic problems. While there is a place for traditional psychological services, there is an equally important need for alternative community programming. Such innovation in other parts of the world has proven to be psychologically therapeutic and nonstigmatizing, leading to personal development. There is no reason why people in the U.S. shouldn't flourish accordingly.

References

Beijing Platform for Action. (1995). Fourth World Conference on Women. Beijing, China.

Blatner, A. (2000). *Foundations of psychodrama: History, theory and practice* (4th Ed.), New York: Springer..

Desjarlais, R., Eisenberg, L., Good, B., and Kleinman, A. (1995), *World mental health: problems and priorities in low-income countries*. New York: Oxford University Press.

Frye, M. (1995). Oppression, in Paula S. Rothenberg, (Ed.), *Race, class, and gender in the United States* (3rd ed., pp.81–84). New York: St. Martin's Press.

Fuller, B. R. (1981). *Critical path*. New York: St. Martin's Press.

Harnois, G. & Gabriel, P. (2000). *Mental health and work: Impact, issues and good practices*. Geneva: World Health Organization.

International Society for Posttraumatic Stress Studies. (July, 1998). UNECOSOC. New York: United Press. Kellerman, P. F. (1992).*Focus on psychodrama: The therapeutic aspects of psychodrama*. London and Philadelphia: Jessica Kingsley-Taylor and Francis Publishers.

Machiavelli, N. (1532/1984). *The Prince*. New York: Bantam Books.

Quannine, J. (1989). *Personal communication*. Dhaka, Bangladesh: Grameen Bank.

Rosenberg, T. (2000, October 26). Looking at poverty, seeing untapped riches. *New York Times*, p. A34.

Schizophrenics Anonymous Online Self-Support Groups (retrieved November 29, 2000.

Shamitz, S. (February 19, 1997). *Engaging refugees and their families*. Presentation by the Director of the Refugee Assistance Program, Adelphi University School of Social Work, Garden City, NY.

Stanton, E. C., Anthony, S. B., and Gage, M. (1985/1881). *History of women suffrage*. Salem, N.H.: The Ayer Company.

Stratigos, S. (2000). *Beijing plus five world women's meeting*. Committee on the Status of Women, E-mail communication. New York: United Nations, July.

Van Wormer, K. (1997). *Social welfare: A world view*. Chicago: Nelson-Hall.

Warren, K.S. (1991). Helminths and health of school-aged children. *The Lancet*, 338:686–687.

World Health Organization and International Labour Organisation (2000). *Mental health & work: Impact, issues and good practices*. Geneva: WHO and ILO.

UNICEF (1989). *The seven sins of development*. New York: United Nations.

Viswanathan, N. & Wetzel, J. W. (1993). Concepts and trends in mental health: A global overview. In P. Mane and K.Y. Gandevia (Eds.) *Mental health in India: Issues and concerns* (pp. 43–69), Bombay: Tata Press.

Wetzel, J. W. (1993). *The world of women: in pursuit of human rights*. United Kingdom: MacMillan Press, Ltd.

Wetzel, J. W. (1994). Depression: Women at risk, co-published simultaneously in Special Edition on Women's Health and Social Work. In Gary Rosenberg, (Ed.), *Social work in health care*, Ed: M. Olson, 19:3/4 1994, 85–108; and: *Women's health and social work: A feminist perspective*, Ed: Gary Rosenberg, Haworth Press, 1994, 85-108.

Wetzel, J. W. (1991a). *Clinical handbook of depression*. New York: Gardner Press.

Wetzel, J. W. (1991b). Universal mental health classification systems: Reclaiming women's experience, *Affilia: Journal of Women and Social Work*, 6(3), 8–31.

World Fellowship for Schizophrenia and Allied Disorders (retrieved November 29, 2000.

World Health Organization and Office of the United Nations High Commissioner of Refugees (1996). *Helping victims of rape and their communities.* Mental Health of Refugees. Unit 9,.123–132.

Yunus, M. & Jolis, A. (1999). *Banker to the poor: Micro-lending and the battle against world poverty.* PublicAffairs.

CHAPTER SEVEN

Social Development: Lessons from the Global South

James Midgley AND Michelle Livermore

S ocial development is a distinctive approach for enhancing people's welfare which can be contrasted with other approaches such as social work, philanthropy, and social administration. Although based on ancient ideas about change and social progress, social development originated in the developing countries of the Global South in the years following the Second World War. Its advocates believe that people's well-being can best be promoted by linking social welfare to economic development. They contend that economic development is a dynamic source of material progress. Provided that it is people centered, sustainable, inclusive and egalitarian, and if harmonized with social welfare policies that foster economic participation, economic development can bring about tangible improvement in well-being for all.

Although it was previously believed that social development is best suited to the nations of the Global South, its relevance to the industrially developed countries has now been recognized. Since the United Nations World Summit on Social Development in Copenhagen in 1995, social development has increasingly been viewed as appropriate to all societies. It has also been suggested that social development's emphasis on harmonizing social and economic policies is particularly relevant to the current economic, political and social realities of the global age.

Social development ideas have been adopted to a limited extent in industrial nations such as the United States. American social workers who have worked abroad, or who have been involved in international development programs have advocated for the adoption of the social development approach. They believe that the social development experiences of the developing nations can be usefully adapted to the needs and circumstances of industrial nations. Indeed, there are signs that social development ideas are now being applied in the United States. The influence of social development is especially evident in projects that seek to promote local economic development to meet the needs of poor communities.

This chapter describes the social development perspective by tracing its origins in the developing world and discussing its key features. It examines the specific programmatic proposals that characterize the social development approach, and considers how they can inform social welfare policies and programs in the United States. Examples of how these ideas have already been applied are also given to illustrate the viability of emulating the social development approach.

The Social Development Approach

As a distinctive approach in social welfare, social development differs from philanthropy, social work, and social administration by emphasizing the importance of a progressive people-centered *development* process in enhancing human well-being. However, the social development approach does not advocate economic development for its own sake but requires that economic development be inclusive and sustainable, and that it results in tangible improvements in social well-being for all (Midgley, 1995). It also proposes that social welfare programs be investment-oriented, and that they enhance people's capabilities to participate in the productive economy (Midgley, 1999).

Today, social development ideas find expression in the advocacy of economic policies that seek, for example, to generate employment, raise incomes, and ensure that workers receive living wages. Proponents of social development urge the adoption of environmentally sensitive economic policies that foster a more egalitarian distribution of income, and provide opportunities for all to participate in the economy and enjoy the benefits of economic life. Since neoliberal ideas currently dominate economic thinking, these proposals are not popular. Nevertheless, they are central to the social development approach and are consistently promoted by social development advocates.

Social development ideas also find expression in the advocacy of what are known as social investment policies and programs. These policies and programs seek to promote the capabilities of poor people and the consumers of social welfare services to participate productively in the economy. Social development thus seeks to augment conventional consumption-based remedial and maintenance social programs with interventions that promote economic development. Although there will always be a need for remedial social services, social development transcends the remedial and maintenance functions of conventional social welfare programs. In addition, its emphasis on social investments and 'productivist' social welfare offers a perspective that may legitimate state welfare at a time when public expenditures on social programs are widely believed to be responsible for economic stagnation.

Historical Evolution

As Midgley (1994) has shown, the term *social development* was coined by British welfare administrators at the end of the colonial era to connote social programs that promote economic development. Because the nationalist movements campaigning for independence believed that economic development was a vital element in the struggle for political independence, the colonial authorities could not ignore the growing pressures for economic self-sufficiency. Economic development was emphasized and, in several colonial territories, the period following the Second World War was characterized by a new commitment to economic planning, the expansion of infrastructure and the promotion of industry. The flow of international aid from the metropolitan nations and multilateral agencies increased to provide the resources needed to foster development.

The new emphasis on development also had implications for the social services. Social welfare programs that had been introduced during the colonial period were modeled on those of the metropolitan nations. They were urban-based, remedial, heavily dependent on residential care and limited in coverage (MacPherson, 1982; Hardiman & Midgley, 1989). Many economic planners and political leaders also believed them to be marginal to the overriding need for economic development (Livingstone, 1969). As it became clear that Western welfare approaches had limited relevance to the needs of the newly

independent countries, new thinking that emphasized the appropri-
ateness of the social services to local social, economic, and cultural
realities gained support. The failure of social programs to reach the
poorest groups and to link social welfare to economic development
also became a prominent issue. Debates on these issues gave rise to
the social development approach.

From formative experiments by British colonial welfare officials in
West Africa with literacy education and other forms of community
development, the concept of social development as the integration of
social welfare with economic development was formulated and popularized. This approach was actively promoted by the United Nations
and other international development agencies. These agencies advocated the adoption of social service programs that were community
based, participatory, and focused on the needs of urban slum dwellers
and the rural poor. In the late 1960s, the international agencies engaged in a major effort to promote social development through economic planning and community participation. Throughout the
developing world, central planning agencies placed far more emphasis on social planning, and community development programs were
expanded. Although these efforts were undermined in the 1970s by
the ascendancy of neoliberal economic and political ideas, Third World
debt, and economic difficulties, the World Summit on Social Development offers a renewed rationale for social welfare which may have
international appeal.

Productivist Social Welfare

As noted earlier, the social development approach requires the adoption of social welfare policies and programs that are investment-
oriented and 'productivist' in that they contribute positively to
economic development (Midgley, 1999). The latter aspect has most
relevance for social workers and social administrators responsible for
the formulation and implementation of welfare policies and programs.
Indeed, this aspect is often regarded by those working in the field of
social welfare as being at the core of the social development approach.

A number of social policies and programs that are investment-
oriented or productivist have now been identified. These include programs that promote human capital formation among poor people and
social welfare clients. It also includes programs that help these clients

find remunerative employment or to engage in productive self-employment. Asset development programs are another key programmatic element of social development. Social development also involves community social programs that facilitate the creation of social capital. Social programs that remove barriers to economic participation and help create an environment conducive to economic development are included as well. Finally, productivist social welfare emphasizes social programs that are cost effective and produce positive rates of return to the economy on social investments.

These types of developmental interventions are being implemented in many parts of the world today, but particularly in the developing countries of the Global South. In these countries, the social development approach has been used to promote human capital and to enhance the capabilities of needy people to participate fully in the economy. It has also been used to promote social capital in poor communities. In addition, social development has helped social welfare clients to find remunerative employment. Finally, social development programs have helped needy people gain access to microcredit and to establish microenterprises. These efforts reveal that the concept of productivist social welfare can be translated into tangible social policies and social programs that, in conjunction with relevant people-centered economic development strategies, enhance the welfare of all.

Social Development in the Global South

The social development approach is being widely used in the developing countries of the Global South today. This does not mean that all developing countries have embraced social development or that it has always been effectively implemented. Nevertheless, social development has been given prominence in many developing countries. It has been applied in several fields of social welfare, but perhaps most effectively in the areas of child welfare, community development, and social assistance. The following examples show how these fields have employed a social development approach.

Child Welfare and Human Capital

The role of human capital in the form of education and skills acquisition is an essential component of development and a vital mechanism for promoting people's welfare (Becker, 1964; Harbison, 1973). For this reason, many developing countries have sought to enhance educational opportunities by establishing schools, colleges, and universities (Psacharopoulos, 1973). While the results of these investments have been impressive, children in rural communities and urban settlements do not always have access to education, and because many poor children are engaged in economic activities to help their families meet subsistence needs, they are excluded from educational opportunities. There is an urgent need for social development programs in the Global South to address this problem if poor children are going to acquire the skills and knowledge to escape a life of poverty (Schultz, 1981).

Although this challenge must be met primarily through the educational system, social welfare programs also have a role to play. Recently, efforts have been made to re-orient conventional child welfare programs in the developing world so that they promote human capital development and contribute positively to economic development. Child welfare services in many developing countries traditionally have been based on a Western, child protective services model in which professionally qualified social workers investigate alleged cases of neglect and abuse, and often remove needy children from their homes placing them in residential facilities. However, social workers in many developing countries have recognized that this approach is an ineffective way of dealing with the problems of child need in societies characterized by mass poverty and deprivation. It is reactive and can only deal with a small number of needy children. It does not address problems such as child labor, a lack of access to schooling, and the deprivations children experience in early childhood. In addition, by focusing on child neglect and abuse, this approach fails to deal with the serious problems of malnutrition and infant death. Conventional child welfare services are also concentrated in the urban areas of developing countries and seldom reach children living in rural areas and particularly remote areas. It is here that needs are often the greatest.

As social workers in developing nations realized that only a small proportion of needy children could be served through conventional child welfare programs, alternative approaches that address the needs of larger numbers of poor children in both urban and rural areas were identified. With the assistance of UNICEF and other international agencies, government social welfare agencies in many developing countries began to promote community-based programs which rely on the active participation of the local community (United Nations Children's Fund, 1982). These programs are centered around a local, neighborhood day care center which is staffed by local people with the support of government social workers and public subsidies. The center provides preschool education, meals, and various other activities that promote women's health, foster prevention and build community solidarity. By promoting human capital through preschool education, nutrition, and health care, this community-based approach to child welfare makes a positive contribution to economic development.

A good example of the adoption of a social development approach in child welfare is the Integrated Child Welfare Services Scheme in India. Many poor villages, as well as squatter and shanty communities in the country's urban areas, are now served by this program. Social workers use community organization techniques to motivate parents and local leaders to establish day care centers for young children. The centers are staffed by paraprofessionals supported by local volunteers under the supervision of professionally qualified social workers. The children are fed, given preschool education, and they participate in organized recreation. Health services such as immunization and weight checks are also provided.

Large numbers of needy children are served and, by emphasizing prevention and social investments, these programs are cost effective. The costs of the program are shared between the government and local community. The government pays for nutritional supplements and the salaries of staff, while the local community provides volunteers and a site for the center. After these day care centers become established and accepted by the community, they extend their programs to offer maternal health education, family planning information, and other programs that enhance the status of women.

India's innovative approach to child welfare is not the only one of its kind in the developing countries of the Global South. However, this program is a good example of how developmental social welfare can help promote human capital. It addresses the pressing social needs of poor families, and at the same time, contributes to development by investing in the human capital of young children. It is also more cost effective than remedial child protective and residential services, and it helps create social conditions conducive to economic development.

Community Development and Social Capital

Because developmental child welfare programs involve the whole community and strengthen social relationships between community members, they also foster the formation of what is known in the sociological literature as *social capital*. Social capital strengthens community networks and, as Professor Robert Putnam of Harvard University and his colleagues have shown, this has a positive impact on economic development (Putnam, Leonardi, & Nanetti, 1993). Social workers in many developing countries help build social networks through community organizing not only to enhance people's participation and mobilize communities to advocate for improved services, but to promote local economic development.

Social workers have been involved in community development projects for many decades. Indeed, it was in West Africa in the 1940s and 1950s that they first sought to transcend the limited remedial focus of urban-based residential and casework services by promoting literacy education and other activities that would have a positive impact on economic development. As noted earlier, it was a result of these activities that the term *social development* came into popular use. Since then, community development has become a key element of social work practice in many African countries and, indeed in Asia, Central and South America, and other regions of the Global South as well (Brokensha & Hodge, 1969).

In many African countries, social workers have mobilized local people to engage in small-scale agricultural activities, construct rural bridges and feeder roads, establish cooperative enterprises, and accumulate community assets. These projects have a direct and positive impact on economic development. Community built and owned feeder roads provide easier access to the markets in larger towns and ensure that farmers get their produce to these markets in a timely way. Community development has also been used to assist women to engage more effectively in agricultural activities and microenterprises and to become economically independent.

Community development has also been used to promote social welfare projects that are productivist and contribute to economic development. Throughout Africa, local people have collaborated with both governmental and nongovernmental agencies to build community centers, schools and clinics, sanitary and other public health facilities, and to provide safe drinking water. The use of community development to provide safe drinking water in many rural areas in Africa has been particularly impressive. Many communities that relied on rivers, streams, and marshes were exposed to the hazard of being infected with waterborne diseases. Community participation has been vital in providing access to clean drinking water. Village people have played an important role by providing labor for the construction of wells and channeling clean water to local communities from unpolluted mountain springs.

Projects of this kind have not only improved public health but have contributed positively to economic development. It is now recognized that healthier people are more productive and able to engage more effectively in the economy. But these projects have also had an impact on economic development through fostering the formation of social capital. By enhancing participation and collaboration, community integration and trust increases, and there is a greater willingness to engage in economic activities and collaborate on projects that promote economic development.

Social Assistance and Microenterprise

Social workers in developing countries have also contributed positively to economic development by assisting low-income and special-needs clients to engage in *productive self-employment*. In particular, they have acquired a good deal of experience in helping clients challenged by disabilities participate in vocational educational programs. They have also helped these clients obtain credit to establish small businesses or microenterprises, as they are also known. These enterprises include both small-scale individual and family-owned businesses, as well as larger cooperatives.

Social workers in Asian countries such as the Philippines have perhaps the most extensive experience of using the microcredit and microenterprise approach. This approach was adopted after the Philippine government abolished its traditional social assistance program in the mid-1970s (Reidy, 1981). As in many other developing countries with social assistance programs, only a small number of needy people, primarily in the cities, could be helped. In addition, payments were small and time-limited. However, because jobs in the formal wage employment sector were scarce, efforts to encourage people to find work were not very successful. For this reason, the government decided to promote microenterprises, which, it believed, offered an innovative opportunity for clients to participate in the productive economy.

While microenterprise activities can take the form of single-proprietor or family-owned businesses, it was suggested previously that they can also operate as cooperatives. There is evidence to show that family participation and the creation of cooperatives are more successful than single-proprietor businesses. Cooperative ventures are particularly well suited to special needs clients, such as the mentally ill or physically disabled, who benefit from working in a mutually supportive environment. In addition, cooperatives can be used to promote wider community involvement and to link microenterprises to local community development programs.

An interesting example of the use of the cooperative principle in microenterprise development is the peer-lending concept. Popularized by the Grameen Bank in Bangladesh, peer lending offers an opportunity for small groups of people with similar needs to collaborate and collectively secure funding for microenterprises (Yunus, 1991). By requiring that loans be obtained jointly, the peer lending principle ensures that individuals are given encouragement and support. This increases the likelihood of long-term success. It is also a particularly useful way of helping those who have historically been oppressed and excluded from economic participation. As is well known, the peer-lending principle has been used quite extensively to assist groups of poor women in developing countries to become economically independent and to function effectively in the productive economy.

Promoting Social Development in the United States

The successful application of social development in child welfare, community development, and social assistance in the developing countries of the Global South offers an opportunity to consider ways in which these approaches can be adapted to fit the needs and circumstances of the industrial nations. While some may argue that these strategies are not well suited to high-income countries, it will be argued here that these approaches are relevant, and that they are particularly useful when implemented in conjunction with community economic development programs focused on low-income areas in these countries.

The following examples seek to show how social development projects are currently being implemented and how they may be further augmented by adapting lessons from abroad.

Child Welfare and Human Capital

The child welfare system in the United States can learn much from the comprehensive initiatives being implemented in the developing nations of the Global South. The current U.S. system is residual and designed to respond to crises. It limits the notion of child welfare to protecting children from harm and removing them from unsatisfactory family environments. Child welfare services, funded largely by the federal government and provided by the states, include child protection, foster and group care, and adoptive services. Although family preservation is an important focus, child welfare programs are still reactive rather than preventive. Since child abuse and neglect often coexist with poverty and deprivation, there is an urgent need to prevent abuse and neglect by addressing the underlying problem of poverty directly. A developmental perspective can inform these attempts.

Fortunately, developmentally focused programs do exist. For example, Head Start targets low-income children and their families for human capital investments. This federally funded preschool program provides children up to the age of five years with language and cognitive development services. These services are designed to help children catch up with their more advantaged peers by the time they reach kindergarten (United States, Department of Health and Human Services, 2000a; United States, House of Representatives, 2000). The program resembles India's Integrated Child Welfare Services Scheme in several respects. In addition to its educational focus, Head Start also provides nutritional meals to children and preventative health care including medical, dental, and mental health services. As in the Integrated Child Welfare Services Scheme, parental involvement is a key component of the Head Start program. Parents are involved in the program as volunteers, service recipients, and employees.

As volunteers, parents participate in program planning and the daily operation of the program. Some also participate in the program's classes on parenting and child development. Additionally, some parents are provided with formal training and certification through the Child Development Associate Program and are subsequently hired as staff in the program (United States House of Representatives, 2000). Thus, in addition to investing in the human capital of children, the program empowers women though education and employment opportunities (United States, Department of Health and Human Services, 2000b; Peters, 1998).

Head Start differs from the Integrated Child Welfare Services Scheme in the extent to which community organization methods are used in its operation, and in the amount of community involvement in the program. This is one lesson that the United States can learn from the Global South. Although located in poor communities where need is greatest, Head Start focuses intervention on the individual child and the family, not the community. By using community organization techniques and focusing on building community solidarity around the human capital development of children and their mothers, India's Integrated Child Welfare Services Scheme provides children and their families a more extensive system of social support. Combining Head Start programs with community-building activities that form group solidarity among mothers and members of the larger community could help bridge part of the socioeconomic divide that characterizes American society today.

Community Development and Social Capital

In Africa, community development strategies have harnessed the local energies and talents of people to build infrastructure that facilitates economic development. These strategies have elicited community participation in the planning and building of community assets such as community centers and schools, business cooperatives, and roads. The strong social relationships that emerge among community members during these activities increases their trust in one another as well as their willingness to participate in future development projects.

Community development professionals in the United States have begun to focus on the development of this type of social capital as a key strategy for enhancing community well-being. Social capital includes the social networks, trust, and norms of reciprocity that exist among people in communities. Although community practice professionals have focused on building social capital for years, they have not always harnessed these resources to contribute directly to economic development (Midgley & Livermore, 1998). One example of a community development initiative that seeks specifically to promote economic development was undertaken by the Local Initiative Support Corporation (LISC). Using consensus organizing techniques, LISC explicitly set out to build community social capital in order to assist community development corporations implement housing and economic development projects (Gittell & Vidal, 1998).

LISC's social capital development strategy involves building internal or 'bonding' social capital within poor communities and then forming 'bridging' social capital that connects poor communities to resources outside local communities. LISC projects are typically implemented through Community Development Corporations (CDCs). In each community, LISC personnel attempt to assemble a board of directors for a CDC that is representative of all segments of the community, intentionally tapping into a wide range of local social networks. Their aim is "to build a broadly based, participatory organization" (Gittell & Vidal, 1998, p. 85). The board is then trained and given the task of planning a real estate development project.

LISC also seeks to link these CDCs to supportive members of the larger community. Establishing links with the local business community is given high priority. These links are essential for the long-term viability of development projects because the CDCs need the private sector to invest capital and to provide political and technical support. Such interactions also help teach residents how to interact with the private sector to enhance their standards of living and affect change.

Prior to establishing itself in a local community, LISC's national program team and its local development team begin to build relationships with the local business community. During the site assessment phase, in which LISC seeks to identify the potential of the local target community to participate, the team visits local business leaders and establishes links. These key players are then involved in the subsequent phases of the project and they are educated about LISC's approach. As the project evolves, the LISC development team works to build relationships between local community members and the private sector. Local technical advisors outside the target community are identified and recruited to help local volunteers with development tasks. Thus, LISC seeks not only to mobilize resources within disadvantaged communities but to help them access external resources through developing bridging social capital (Gittell & Vidal, 1998).

Community development efforts in the United States, such as LISC, seek to develop social capital in local communities as a part of a community development strategy. However, they are typically concerned with private housing and individually-owned businesses. Compared with their counterparts in the Global South, these projects are limited and tend to be excessively focused on individual enterprise rather than cooperative endeavors. While the culture of the United States is noted for its individualism, this culture does not dominate all communities in this country. Indeed, some minority communities have cooperative, self-help traditions that would readily adopt the more collaborative strategies implemented in developing countries. There is no doubt that community development efforts in the United States can learn from cooperative business activities and other community asset building initiatives that are the focus of community development projects in the developing world.

Social Assistance and Microenterprise

As noted earlier, helping low-income and special needs clients participate in the economy is another strategy that social workers can use to ensure that social welfare contributes to economic development. Microcredit and microenterprise programs are already being used in the United States, although on a limited basis, to help individuals living in poor areas and those receiving public assistance become self-sufficient. Although, as Servon (1999) notes, the Model Cities program and the Small Business Administration's Equal Opportunity Loans program have influenced the creation of microenterprise development programs in the United States since the 1960s, the expansion of microenterprise and microcredit programs has also been significantly affected by the diffusion of information about such programs in the Global South.

One example of a microenterprise program explicitly based on the experiences of the developing countries is Working Capital. Its founder, Jeffery Ashe, worked for ACCION International. ACCION International is an umbrella organization for microfinance institutions in developing countries that has, for the past 25 years, provided microloans to assist individuals living in poverty to start or expand their own businesses (ACCION International, 2001).

Ashe was particularly impressed with an organization called the Foundation for International Assistance (FINCA), which exists in several Latin American countries, and he has used the FINCA model to guide Working Capital's activities in the United States (Servon, 1999). The FINCA model provides both loans and training through peer groups. It gives maximum responsibility to borrowers and utilizes existing community resources for training. The peer group process follows six distinct stages. First, business and personal profiles of each individual are discussed. Then participants prepare initial income statements and loan applications. Next, the peer group develops bylaws and elects officers. The officers are trained and loan applications are reviewed. Finally, checks are distributed and six-month action plans are developed. This process is vital because it helps group members develop relationships that are essential to program success (Servon, 1999).

Although the group lending approach has been successful, some challenges and difficulties have to be overcome. The individualism that is so prevalent in the United States makes the group-based lending model difficult for some. Additionally, operating a microenterprise is more challenging in the United States because of the complexity of the formal economy and the smaller scale and relative inaccessibility of the informal economy in comparison with the Global South. These factors increase the amount of capital and specific knowledge needed to start a business, raising the cost of initiating such programs (Servon, 1999).

Nevertheless, Working Capital now operates in six states and successfully promotes a peer-based microenterprise approach. It is a good example of the adaptation of an innovation from the developing world that seeks to apply the microenterprise approach within the context of a social development model.

Conclusion: The Benefit of Adapting Social Development

As these examples reveal, social development ideas have already been implemented in the United States and have further potential to influence social policy in positive ways. The examples cited also show that existing programs can be further augmented by understanding how they operate in the Global South and, in particular, how they make use of a community rather than individualistic approach to social welfare.

However, these programs also need to be related to the wider economic and social context. It was argued earlier that social development does not merely involve the inclusion of poor people and individual social welfare clients in the productive economy. It requires substantive modifications to the way the economic system functions. It rejects the idea that the relentless pursuit of profits will somehow result in tangible improvements for all. Social development's macro-framework requires that social programs operate within a wider economic context that is sustainable and people-centered. Of course, this aspect of the social development approach will be hardest to implement.

Nevertheless, social development has the potential to provide a new rationale for government intervention in social welfare in the United States. At a time when traditional government social programs are widely believed to be wasteful, ineffective, and harmful to the nation's economy, the argument that these programs can contribute positively to economic development may have electoral appeal. The trend towards retrenchment and even the abolition of government involvement can be countered by a commitment to promoting developmental forms of social welfare that enhance economic participation and promote economic development.

Despite America's unique cultural, economic, and social situation, the principles of social development outlined earlier are relevant in a local context. Indeed, there is much in the social development approach that is compatible with national cultural themes. For example, the idea of economic participation as an effective means of meeting social needs is a fundamental belief in American society. Most individuals provide for themselves and their families through engaging in economic activities and few would oppose government efforts to promote the engagement of others in productive and remunerative employment. The developmental perspective recognizes the potential and desire of those who are excluded from the economic mainstream to participate in the economy and, in this way, to improve their standards of living.

The notion of social investments that enhance what Amartya Sen (1985, 1999) calls the "capabilities" of individuals to function effectively in the economy will also resonate with many Americans. Although some will dismiss the need for government intervention and stress the importance of unaided individual effort and self-reliance, the idea that government should help people become self-sufficient goes back to the nation's founding and will resonate with many ordinary citizens. As Zundel (2000) reveals, Americans historically have benefited from what he calls the "civic republican tradition" by which government provided homesteads for settlers, mortgage relief for homeowners, and a variety of fiscal incentives and subsidies to encourage savings. Most Americans will recognize that public education, tax credits, and other supports have improved the quality of their lives and enhanced their welfare. Many would recognize the need for similar benefits which can help fellow citizens realize their potential.

The role of social development in enhancing community solidarity will also have appeal. Many Americans believe that the bonds of solidarity which characterized traditional community life have weakened over the years. Indeed, the loss of community has been a recurrent theme in social science writing in the United States, and has found recent expression in the work of Etzioni (1993), Wilson (1987), and Putnam (1995, 1996), among others. The segregation of the poor and the association of poverty with race and other sources of differentiation have created a serious problem of exclusion and isolation that is not only socially but economically costly. The potential of a social development approach to promote economic participation and foster social integration among those who are currently on the margins of the productive economy deserves consideration.

It must, of course, be recognized that these sentiments will not be universally shared and that the country's belief in unfettered individualism continues to have appeal. Current political realities will also impede efforts to promote social development. The antipathy to government intervention which characterizes American society today will not rapidly evaporate and there will be little support for the economic interventionism that accompanies a people-centered social development approach. Similarly, issues of race and discrimination will continue to challenge social development's potential to foster economic and social inclusion. Nevertheless, the implementation of social development projects may help to popularize its values and create new opportunities for government to play a more positive role in social welfare in the future.

References

ACCION International (2001). Program Description. http://www.accion.org/press/meidakit.asp.

Becker, G. (1964) *Human capital: A theoretical and empirical analysis with special reference to education.* New York: Columbia University Press.

Brokensha, D., & Hodge, P. (1969). *Community development: An interpretation.* San Francisco, CA: Chandler.

Etzioni, A. (1993). *The spirit of community: Rights, responsibilities and the communitarian agenda.* New York: Crown.

Gittell, R., & Vidal, A. (1998). *Community organizing: Building social capital as a development strategy.* Thousand Oaks, CA: Sage Publications.

Harbison, F. H. (1973). *Human resources as the wealth of nations.* London: Oxford University Press.

Hardiman, M., & Midgley, J. (1989). *The social dimensions of development: Social policy and planning in the Third World.* (Rev. ed.) Aldershot: Gower.

Livingston, A. (1969). *Social policy in developing countries.* London: Routledge & Kegan Paul.

MacPherson, S. (1982). *Social policy in the Third World.* Brighton: Wheatsheaf.

Midgley, J. (1994). Defining social development: Historical trends and conceptual formulations. *Social Development Issues,* 16 (3), 3–19.

Midgley, J. (1995). *Social development: The developmental perspective in social welfare.* Thousand Oaks, CA: Sage Publications.

Midgley, J. (1999). Growth, redistribution and welfare: Towards social investment. *Social Service Review,* 77(1): 3–21.

Midgley, J. & Livermore, M. (1998). Social capital and local economic development: Implications for community social work practice. *Journal of Community Practice,* 5(1/2): 29–40.

Peters, B. J. (1998). *The Head Start mother: Low-income mothers' empowerment through participation.* New York: Garland Publishing.

Psacharopoulos, G. (1973). *Returns to education: An international comparison.* Amsterdam: Elsevier.

Putnam, R. (1995). Bowling alone: America's declining social capital, *Journal of Democracy,* 6, 65–78.

Putnam, R. (1996). The strange disappearance of civic America, *American Prospect,* Winter, 34–48.

Putnam, R. D., with Leonardi, R. & Nanetti, R. Y. (1993) *Making democracy work: Civic traditions in modern Italy.* Princeton: Princeton University Press.

Reidy, A. (1981). Welfarists in the market. *International Social Work,* 24(2): 36–46.

Schultz, T. W. (1981). *Investing in people*. Berkeley, CA: University of California Press.

Sen, A. (1985). *Commodities and capabilities*. Amsterdam: North-Holland.

Sen, A. (1999). *Development as freedom*. New York: Knopf.

Servon, L. J. (1999). *Bootstrap capital: Microenterprises and the American poor*. Washington D.C.: The Brookings Institution.

United Nations Children's Fund (1982). Popular participation in basic services: Lessons learned through UNICEF's experience, *Assignment Children*, 59/60 (1) 121–132.

United States, Department of Health and Human Services, (2000a). Head start: general information. Washington, D.C. (http://www2.acf.dhhs.gov/programs/hsb/about/mission.htm).

United States, Department of Health and Human Services (DHHS). (2000b). *2000 Head Start Fact Sheet*. Washington, DC. (http://www2.acf.dhhs.gov/programs/hsb/research/00_hsfs.html).

United States House of Representatives, Committee of Way and Means (2000). *The 2000 Green Book*. Washington, DC: (http://aspe.hhs.gov/2000gb.)

Wilson, W. J. (1987). *The truly disadvantaged: The inner city, the underclass and public policy*. Chicago: University of Chicago Press.

Yunus, M. (1991). *Grameen Bank: Experiences and reflections*. Dhaka: Grameen Bank.

Zundel, A. F. (2000). *Declarations of dependency: The civic republican tradition in U.S. poverty policy*. Albany, NY: State University of New York Press.

CHAPTER EIGHT

International Social Welfare Treaties and Conventions: Implications for the United States

Elizabeth Lightfoot

The previous chapters of this book have shown that social administrators and policymakers in the United States can benefit from the experiences of countries which have introduced a variety of innovations in the fields of child welfare, the care of the elderly, mental health, social security, and other social welfare fields. Indeed, these chapters have provided interesting examples of how American social welfare has already been informed by the experiences of these countries. They have also alluded to the ways in which the process of learning from abroad operates. Information has been exchanged through reports and official publications, international meetings, study tours, academic publications, and personal contacts. Usually, the adoption of innovations from abroad has not involved the mechanical replication of policies and programs but has fostered adaptations in which innovations or elements of innovations have been incrementally implemented.

Welfare innovations can also be diffused in a more formal way. For example, governments and non-profit organizations may establish official links with their counterparts in other countries to share information and experiences and to review each other's programs. They may also collaborate to establish joint programs. Another important mechanism involves the signing and ratification of international treaties and conventions. These policy instruments are now widely used not only to muster the support of the world's nation states for particular economic, social and political purposes but to establish international standards which can promote best practices, enhance programs and ensure that social needs are met. While some of these treaties, such as the *United Nations Declaration on Human Rights,* are very well known and institutionalized in everyday thinking, others are still unfamiliar. But all have the potential to play a major role in internationalizing social welfare innovations and ensuring that acceptable standards of provision are met. This role is augmented by the fact that international treaties and conventions have, theoretically at least, the force of international law.

This chapter examines some of the most important international treaties and conventions and considers their role in promoting the diffusion of innovations in a variety of social welfare fields. It describes the leading organizations responsible for giving leadership in drafting and promoting the adoption of the instruments. It then focuses on the different types of treaties and conventions that have been formulated. The discussion is linked to broader issues of social rights and international law.

The chapter also shows that the government of the United States has signed many of these international treaties and conventions. However, for various reasons, difficulties have been experienced with regard to ratification. The chapter concludes with a discussion of this problem. We hope that the situation will improve and that the United States will play a more active role in promoting the adoption of international social welfare standards commensurate with its position as a world power.

International Law and Social Welfare

Before the establishment of the United Nations, international organizations, such as the League of Nations, were not concerned so much with domestic policy as they were with diffusing and preventing external conflicts between nations (Driscoll, 1989). Only exceptional cases, such as the denial of basic rights to aliens or the existence of slavery, warranted domestic intervention by external sources in the form of treaties or international agreements (Driscoll, 1989). However, the post-World War II formation of the United Nations in 1945 and the subsequent adoption of the United Nations Universal Declaration of Human Rights in 1948 has changed the scope of international organizations to include a strong focus on the rights of individuals within countries. In the latter half of the twentieth century, the United Nations and regional international organizations, such as the Council on Europe and the Organization of American States, exhibited an increasing interest in the civil, political, social, cultural and economic rights of individuals within countries. The following section will present the general structure of international law and show how international law is applicable to domestic social welfare.

International law differs from domestic law, as it is not imposed on nations by an international legislature but is rather an understanding between sovereign nations. The sources of international law are either international customs or international agreements. Customary international law is a practice followed by nations because they feel legally obligated. For a general custom to be legally obligating, it must be a custom that has had widespread, long-term adherence by many nations, and have some evidence of *opinio juris*, or a feeling of obligation or belief that adherence is mandatory (Hillier, 1994). The following practices are examples of violations of customary international law: genocide; slavery; murder or causing the disappearance of individuals (not including executions after a fair trial); torture and other cruel, inhuman or degrading treatment; prolonged arbitrary detention; and systematic racial discrimination (Hillier, 1994). Customary international law is binding on all nations, though occasionally a nation who has consistently objected to a rule will not be bound by it (Hillier, 1994).

International treaties are as binding as customary law (Hillier, 1994). International treaties are written agreements between one or more nations are governed by international law (Hillier, 1994). International treaties often simply reflect the codification of international customary law (United Nations, 1999). The terminology association with international treaties can be confusing, as treaties can be referred to as treaties, covenants, accords, statutes, protocols, and agreements, among other titles (United Nations, 1999). While the titles differ, the legal force of international treaties varies not so much with the different titles of the agreement, but on the type of agreement, the language within the agreement, and the varying interpretations of the agreement.

General International Agreements

General international agreements, such as titled treaties, conventions or covenants, are usually the most broad and most binding, as they contain enforcement procedures that ensure ratifying nations comply with the law. The process of adopting a treaty can vary, but generally a multilateral treaty involves first a two-thirds vote by the United Nations General Assembly to adopt the form and proposed text of a treaty. Member nations can then sign a treaty, but this signature only signifies a that a nation will continue through with the ratification process. By ratifying a treaty, a nation is indicating that it consents to be bound by that treaty (United Nations, 1999). Ratification is at the discretion of member nations, so nations have developed their own ratification protocols. For example, in the United Kingdom treaties are ratified by a signature of the monarch without a requirement of parliamentary action (Hillier, 1994), while in the United States ratification involves the approval in the Senate by a two-thirds majority vote. When a fixed number of member nations have ratified a treaty, the treaty is then entered into force. The most sweeping, binding human rights treaties that cover social welfare issues are The International Covenant on Economic, Social and Cultural Rights (ICESCR) and the International Covenant on Civil and Political Rights (ICCPR), both signed in 1966 (See Table A).

Specialized International Agreements

While general international agreements apply equally to all people, specialized international agreements are directed to the protection of particular rights or particular groups of people. These agreements are usually borne out of the specialized agencies of the United Nations, such as the World Health Organization (WHO) or the United Nations International Children's Emergency Fund (UNICEF). For example, UNICEF spearheaded the ten-year process of adopting the Convention on the Rights of the Child, which seeks to protect and safeguard children under the age of 18 (United Nations, 1989). These specialized agreements, which have been proliferating, are ratified in the same way as global agreements and are equally binding.

Declarations and resolutions are international agreements that are not designed to be legally binding, but reflect a general consensus

Table A.

General International Agreements (*The International Bill of Human Rights*)	Major Specialized International Agreements	Sampling of 'Non-Binding' International Agreements	Major Regional International Agreements	Practices Banned by International Customary Law
• Universal Declaration of Human Rights (1948)[a] • International Covenant on Civil and Political Rights (1966) • International Covenant on Economic, Social and Cultural Rights (1966) • Optional Protocol to the ICCPR (1976) • Second Optional Protocol to the ICCPR aiming at the abolition of the death penalty (1989)	• Convention on the Elimination of Racial Discrimination (1966) • Convention on the Elimination of Discrimination Against Women (1979) • Convention on the Rights of the Child (1989) • International Convention on the Protection of the Rights of All Migrant Workers and Their Families (1990)	• Declaration on the Rights of Mentally Retarded Persons (1971) • Declaration on the Rights of Disabled Persons (1975) • Universal Declaration on the Eradication of Hunger & Malnutrition (1974) • Declaration on the Elimination of Violence Against Women (1993) • Guidelines for the Prevention of Juvenile Delinquency "The Riyadh Guidelines" (1990)	• American Convention On Human Rights, "Pact of San Jose" (1969) • European Convention for the Protection of Human Rights and Fundamental Freedoms (1950) • African Charter on Human and People's Rights (1981)	• Genocide • Slavery • Murder or disappearance • Torture or other cruel, inhuman, or degrading treatment • Prolonged arbitrary detention • Systematic racial discrimination

a. The Universal Declaration on Human Rights (1948) is considered to be binding due to customary law (United Nations, 2000).

among member nations of the United Nations. These international agreements are not usually binding on member nations, as they do not require ratification by individual nations, but rather are accepted by a majority vote of the United Nations General Assembly or one of its subsidiary organs, such as WHO or the International Labour Organization. In the area of human rights, declarations can be especially weak due to the language used in the documents, which often stresses the "encouraging" and "assisting in the realization of" various human rights, rather than mandating or requiring their realization (Driscoll, 1989). Nonetheless, declarations can be effective tools in influencing national policy. First, they can give precedence for future binding international agreements. For example, the Universal Declaration on the Rights of the Child signed in 1948 was not legally binding, but gave rise to the binding Convention on the Rights of the Child adopted nearly forty years later. The declarations themselves can also have a large impact on customary international law, and in fact, may become the embodiment of such law. For example, the Universal Declaration on Human Rights (UDHR), the premiere human rights declaration passed in 1948, has now become effectively binding on all member nations as international customary law (United Nations, 1999).

Even if a binding international agreement, such as the ICCPR, is ratified, there are questions as to how binding these agreements can be concerning domestic issues. First, nations are not required to agree to all aspects of a treaty. A nation can put "reservations" on a treaty, which allows it to accept a treaty in general, but to object to certain provisions which it does not want to be bound to. For example, when the United States finally ratified the ICCPR in 1992, it put a number of reservations on the ratification, including refusing to accept the prohibition on juvenile execution (Levesque, 1996). Even if a nation does not put a reservation on an international agreement, there is some doubt as to whether a violation of a treaty can be enforced. In fact, the United Nations Charter has a domestic jurisdiction clause which states that "nothing contained in the present Charter shall authorize the United Nations to intervene in matters which are essentially within the domestic jurisdiction of any State. . ." (United Nations, 1945, Article 2.7). However, the Permanent Court of International Justice has found that domestic violations of this Charter are, in fact, matters of international concern (Driscoll, 1989; United Nations Department of Public Information, 1987b). The main underpinning of these international agreements is that nations give consent to be bound by them (Eisenberg, 1988). The Court of International Justice believes countries are bound to these agreements by customary law (United Nations Department of Public Information, 1987a). Some have argued, though, that because the United Nation is not a world legislature, the agreements are not given the same careful consideration they would receive if they were domestic laws, and thus should not be considered binding (Eisenberg, 1988).

Regardless of whether these international agreements are truly legally binding for individual nations, many of these agreements have been far from successful in guaranteeing the rights they aim to protect (LaQueur & Rubin, 1989). Most nations are more focused on their own domestic or regional political realities rather than on broader international agreements. In addition, the structuring of the enforcement procedures in the United Nations requires, in most cases, an accusation of a rights violation from another country. Most nations are unwilling to bring rights violations charges against other nations for political reasons (Driscoll, 1989).

Regional International Agreements

A number of regional agreements also protect human rights, and it has been suggested that regional agreements have been heretofore more successful than general United Nations agreements (Hillier, 1994). For example, in Europe, the European Convention on Human Rights and Fundamental Rights (ECHR), which was adopted in 1950 by the Council of Europe, lists a number of political and civil rights similar to those contained in the United Nations UDHR, such as the right to life; freedom from torture, inhuman, or degrading punishment; freedom from slavery and forced labor; and freedom of thought, conscience, and religion (ECHR, 1950). However, unlike the UDHR, the ECHR is binding to member nations, and allows for both nations and individuals who feel their rights have been violated to bring a complaint to the European Commission of Human Rights.

Similarly, the American Convention on Human Rights, commonly known as the "Pact of San Jose, Costa Rica," adopted in 1969, is closely modeled on the United Nations Declaration of Human Rights. However, the Pact of San Jose details the specifics of the rights protected, such as defining the right to life as including banning capital punishment for minors, persons over age 70, and pregnant women; banning capital punishment for political crimes; and banning the expansion of capital punishment to crimes not currently covered (OAS, 1969, Chapter 2, article 4, sections 4, 5). The Pact of San Jose also establishes an Inter-American Court of Human Rights and provides the framework for how the Inter-American Commission On Human Rights will monitor human rights in the Americas. The Commission monitors individual claims as well as claims made by other countries. Most nations in the Americas have ratified the Pact of San Jose, with the United States a notable exception.

Generations of Rights

The rights protected by international agreements have direct relevance to the field of social welfare, particularly in the social work core areas of promoting social justice and the dignity and worth of individuals (National Association of Social Workers, 1999). There are three types of "rights" protected by international law, usually called *first, second,* and *third generations* of rights (Hillier, 1994). All three promote aspects of social welfare.

First generation rights are the classically liberal ideas of political and civil rights that are the foundation of Western democracies such as the United States. These first generation rights are primarily rights of political freedom and liberty, focusing on "negative" rights, or the freedom "from," rather than positive rights, or the "right to." These first generation negative rights include the right to life, liberty, and security of person; freedom of thought, conscience, and religion; freedom of association; and freedom from torture. While first generation rights are generally negative rights, there are several notions of positive first generation rights as well, including the right to a fair and public trial, the right to free elections, and the right to asylum from persecution. The first generation of rights are embodied in the ICCPR, the second of the three-part International Bill of Rights adopted by the United Nations in 1966. These first generation rights are consistent with the core social work value of social justice recognized in the NASW Code of Ethics, specifically the values of ending discrimination and ensuring public participation (NASW, 1999).

Second generation rights go beyond the rights to liberty and free-dom, and promote social, economic, and cultural rights. As opposed to the predominance of negative rights in the first generation, second generation rights are positive rights, or the "rights to." These rights are embodied in the ICESCR, the third part of the *International Bill of Rights*. Included in the ICESCR are the rights to social security, to work and to protection against unemployment, to a standard of living adequate for health and well-being, and to education. These rights call for state intervention to promote social equity, and suggest that there is a minimum standard of living that must be ensured for all people. The wording of the ICESCR only calls for nations to "recognize" these rights, and thus is more difficult to enforce than the ICCPR rights. These rights are clearly within the social welfare tradition of promoting social justice, and are clearly stated in the NASW Code of Ethics: "all people have equal access to the resources, employment, services, and opportunities they require to meet their basic human needs and to develop fully" (NASW, 1999, 6.04).

Third generation rights are those which go beyond individual rights, and can be viewed as "people's rights" (Hillier, 1994, 318) or community rights. These rights include the right to social development and the right to self determination, and can be argued to extend to the right to a healthy environment, the right to peace, and the right to humanitarian aid (Weston, 1986). While third generation rights are often disputed as being unenforceable and thus invalid, these rights are also consistent with the values of social welfare that go beyond national equity and equality, to address the needs and self-determination of individuals, groups, and communities on a global basis.

Sample Treaties

While the ICCPR and the ICESCR promote broad international rights related to social welfare issues, a number of specialized international agreements relate specifically to promoting the rights and social welfare of particular groups of people. The following section will briefly describe two specialized international agreements that focus on social welfare issues—the Convention on the Rights of the Child and the Convention on the Elimination of All Forms of Discrimination against Women. Other specialized international agreements can be found in table A.

Convention on the Rights of the Child

The Convention on the Rights of the Child (CRC) had its impetus in the nonbinding Declaration of the Rights of the Child, adopted in 1959 by the United Nations General Assembly, which laid out the basic principles for protecting children's rights. The CRC was adopted in 1989 and entered into law in 1990 (United Nations, 1990). It is the most widely ratified international human rights treaty, and currently only the United States and Somalia have not yet ratified it. The CRC promotes a variety of human rights for children under the age of 18 in the form of 42 substantive articles. These articles promote both first and second generation rights. The rights protected all have a strong emphasis on promoting the best interests of the child and parental rights, seek to calibrate the rights based on the child's maturity, and seek a balance between granting freedoms for children while protecting children from harm (Korr et al., 1994).

Both the first and the second generation rights in the CRC have strong implications for social welfare. Examples of the first generation rights protected by the CRC include the right to life; freedom of expression; the right to non-separation from parents without judicial review; freedom from abuse and neglect; freedom from economic and sexual exploitation; and freedom from torture, life imprisonment, and capital punishment. These rights fit squarely within the realm of social welfare, with direct implications for child protection, adoption, education and juvenile justice. The CRC's second generation protections include the right to health care, social security, an adequate standard of living, education, and access to child care for parents. These rights cover the major areas of social welfare provision, and have major implications for the structure of social service provisions in ratifying nations.

The rights listed in the CRC are intended to provide a framework for individual nations to set goals for changing its laws, services, and practices in regards to children's issues. The treaty itself was designed to be adaptable to each individual nation's needs, and although it did not specify which practices countries must adopt, it established a reporting mechanism by which countries can measure their progress towards reaching their goals. As of 1996, UNICEF reported that of reporting nations, 35 had passed new laws or amended existing laws to conform to the CRC. Examples of this new legislation include

Germany's adoption of legislation to expand the law to make sexual abuse of children abroad and the possession of pornographic materials illegal; Burkina Faso's revision of child labor legislation to bring it into line with the CRC; Romania's amendment of adoption laws to require training for magistrates for juvenile delinquency and child abuse cases and to reform the child protection system; and Sri Lanka's passage of new legislation banning child labor (UNICEF, 1996). In addition, 25 nations have created bodies to monitor progress on the Convention (UNICEF, 1996).

The Convention on the Elimination of All Forms of Discrimination against Women

Another specialized international agreement is the Convention on the Elimination of All Forms of Discrimination against Women (CEDAW), which was adopted by the United Nations General Assembly in 1979 and entered into force in 1981. The CEDAW consists of a preamble and 30 substantive articles which define discrimination against women and set an agenda for national action to end such discrimination (website). It is often referred to as an international bill of rights for women (website). As of 2003, CEDAW has been ratified by 175 countries, with the notable exceptions of Iran, Somalia, Sudan, the United Arab Emirates, the United States, and Tonga (UN Division for the Advancement of Women, 2000). As the CRC does for children, the CEDAW protects both first and second generation rights of women. First generation rights include the rights to vote and hold office; the right to equal pay for equal work; the right to equality in marriage; and freedom from discrimination in the areas of employment, education, political participation, and health care. Second generation rights include the right of appropriate medical services in connection with pregnancy; the right to family benefits; the right to maternity leave with pay; the right to bank loans, mortgages, and other forms of financial credit; the right to social security; and the right to paid leave. CEDAW is also the only international agreement that protects the reproductive rights of women (UN Division for the Advancement of Women, 2000).

Like the CRC, the rights outlined in the CEDAW are designed for individual nations to use when setting goals and priorities for women's rights. At the Fourth World Conference on Women, held in Beijing in

1995, the lack of respect for the human rights of women as embodied in the CEDAW was one of the main areas of concern. However, the United Nations Committee on the Elimination of Discrimination against Women has reported notable progress by some individual nations in meeting their goals of implementing CEDAW through new policies and outreach activities. Examples of this policy progress include the granting of the right to vote for women in Oman; the elimination of discrimination against women in nationality laws in Monaco and the Republic of Korea; the passage of legislation banning genital mutilation in Ghana and Senegal; the establishment of family courts in Iran and Nepal; and amendments in the Constitution to gurantee equality between men and women by Eritrea, Ethiopia, Morocco, and Poland. Examples of outreach include the implementation of legal education programs focusing on the rights of women in a number of countries, the dissemination of information regarding women's rights, and support of nongovernmental women's organizations (United Nations, 2000).

Influence of International Treaties on the United States

As discussed earlier, international agreements address key social welfare issues and can have a strong legislative impact on domestic social welfare policy within nations. However, the United States has not ratified many international human rights agreements, and those it has ratified, it has ratified with significant reservations limiting the enforceability of these agreements. This section will discuss the difficulties in ratifying human rights agreements in the United States and the current and potential impact of international agreements in the United States.

Ratification Fights

The United States historically has been slow to ratify human rights treaties (Kaufman, 1990). This is partially due to the structure of the ratification process in the United States. In the United States, a ratified treaty becomes part of the supreme law of the land, with weight equal to federal law. Ratification of treaties requires a Senate majority of two-thirds. Because the Senate structure allows for political minorities to delay legislation, treaty opponents are often able to stall legislation for years. And before a vote is taken, there is a thorough evaluation of the constitutionality and any potential impacts of a treaty, which can also take years. These procedural barriers can cause great delays, even among treaties that are well supported. For example, the Genocide Convention, originally adopted by the United Nations General Assembly in 1948, was not ratified by the United States Senate until 1986, and implementing legislation was not enacted until 1989 (LeBlanc, 1991). Similarly, the ICCPR of 1966, with which the United States was deeply involved in authoring and fits well with the liberalism inherent in its Constitution, was not signed by the United States until 1977, and not ratified until 1992.

As ratified treaties are treated as federal law in the United States, they are treated seriously. However, a treaty can be either *self-executing* or *non-self-executing*. A self-executing treaty is a treaty which upon ratification becomes federal law, without requiring any additional legislation. Treaties that are non-self-executing require additional legislation after ratification to be implemented. While there is much confusion regarding when a treaty should be considered non-self-executing, there are generally four recognized reasons why additional implementing legislation would be necessary in the United States: 1) if the parties to the treaty intend for the treaty to be accomplished through national legislation, 2) if the treaty issues address Constitutional matters, 3) if the treaty requires a change in law that Constitutionally necessitates a legislative action, and 4) if there are no legal rights of action in the treaty for potential plaintiffs to seek remedy in the courts (Vasquez, 1995). There is historical precedence for considering all treaties to be non-self-executing in the United States, which dates back to the proposed Bricker Amendment to the Constitution in the 1950s requiring all treaties to be non-self-executing, as a means to avoid ending discrimination and segregation through international treaty (Heckin, 1995). While this amendment was not adopted, the preference for non-self-executing treaties has persisted (Henkin, 1995). Indeed, many have argued that the United States, by refusing to ratify agreements which do not already have a legislative and judicial structure for enforcing, is being more responsible than known rights violators who ratify agreements with little intention of honoring them (Horowitz, 1993).

The United States also has strong political groups opposed to the passage of treaties for a variety of reasons, most notably because they are fearful of United Nations involvement in domestic affairs. These groups have lobbied heavily to oppose international treaties in the 1990s. For example, there was a widespread effort among conservative groups in the United States to block the passage of the CRC (Limber & Wilcox, 1996). The main concerns of these groups were that the ratification of the CRC would usurp national and state sovereignty, undermine parental authority, allow and encourage children to sue parents, allow and encourage children to have abortions, and enable the United Nations to dictate how parents raise and teach their children (UNICEF, US). These groups raised particular concerns about how the CRC could potentially prohibit private schools, permit abortions, and allow children freedom from parental control, even suggesting that the CRC protects a child's right to view pornography or refusal to attend church (Kilbourne, 1996). These conservative concerns were echoed in the Senate by the then-Chair of the Senate Committee on Foreign Relations, Jesse Helms, who outlined a number of reasons he objected to ratification of the CRC, including that the CRC "is incompatible with the God-given right and responsibility of parents to raise their children . . . [and] . . . has the potential to severely restrict States and the Federal Government in their efforts to protect children and to enhance family life" (S. Res 133, 1995).

Despite these obstacles, four treaties have been ratified in the United States in recent years, after decades of delay (See Table B). The United States ratified the Genocide Convention in 1989, the International Covenant on Civil and Political Rights in 1992, the Convention against Torture in 1994, and the International Convention on the Elimination of All Forms of Racial Discrimination in 1994. The Clinton Administration was also keen on ratifying the CEDAW, the CRC, and the ICESCR, but was thwarted by the Senate (Henkin, 1995). Despite the apparent progress in the last decade, the ratified treaties all had significant reservations placed on them, including reservations that the ratified treaties will not require any change in any existing United States law or practice, that the United States will not carry out any treaty obligation inconsistent with the United States Constitution, that the United States will not be subject to adjudication by the International Court of Justice, that states rather than the federal government should be responsible for implementing any treaty, and that all human rights treaties should be non-self-executing (Henkin, 1995). Thus, the ratification of human rights treaties by the United States signifies only a limited adherence to the articles of the treaties.

Table B. Major Human Rights Treaties Ratified by the United States

Major Human Rights Treaty	Year entered into force by the United Nations General Assembly	Year Ratified/ Accessioned by the United States
Slavery Convention	1927	3/21/29
Convention on the Prevention and Punishment of the Crime of Genocide	1951	11/25/88
International Covenant on Civil and Political Rights (ICCPR)	1966	6/08/92
Convention on the Elimination on All Forms of Racial Discrimination (CERD)	1965	10/21/94
Convention against Torture and Other Cruel, Inhuman or Degrading Treatment or Punishment (Torture Convention)	1984	10/21/94

Potential Impacts of International Agreements

The United States has some of the most sweeping civil and political rights laws in the world, yet these laws still have not eliminated discrimination, poverty, and abuse. International agreements can be a tool for the federal government or activists to address these persisting problems. While the United States has lagged behind in ratifying international agreements, these agreements can still have a large impact on social welfare policy. The following discussion will address how U.S. policy would be affected by ratifying treaties or removing significant reservations from ratified treaties, by ratifying more treaties while including reservations, or even without ratifying any subsequent treaties.

Impact of Ratified Treaties without Reservations

The clearest way for international treaties to influence social welfare policy and practice in the United States is for the U.S. to ratify the numerous human rights treaties it has not acted upon, and to remove the significant reservations it has placed on the five rights treaties it has ratified. This would benefit the United States in a number of ways. First, the ratification and removal of reservations on human rights treaties would symbolically demonstrate to the international community that the United States is committed to promoting social justice for all its citizens. This would demonstrate the United States government's role as a world leader in human rights (U.S. Fund for UNICEF, 1998), and give the United States moral authority it currently lacks to protest human rights abuses in other nations. Second, the ratification of treaties could influence the framing of social welfare issues. For example, ratifying the CRC could lead to a change in American society's perception of children. The CRC can reframe our view of the role of parental rights, with a new emphasis on the best interests of the child and the need for support for families, including state intervention (Levesque, 1996). Indeed, examples from abroad have shown that the CRC is changing how practitioners in some countries view children (Nyland, 1999). Third, ratification of treaties could also influence changes in legislation. Indeed, as ratified self-executing treaties without reservations are the supreme law of the land, they in effect become law. When ratifying a treaty, the United States will pass implementing legislation to agree with the treaty. Further, as human rights treaties often provide general guidelines rather than specific details for how rights must be implemented domestically, these guidelines could serve as a tool to influence changes in legislation. Fourth, if treaties were ratified, then the treaties could be used as a litigation tool in both national and international courts.

Impact of Ratified Treaties with Significant Reservations

Since all of the human rights treaties adopted by the United States have been adopted with the reservation that they are non-self-executing and are thus NOT the supreme law of the land, then human rights laws in this country effectively have no teeth. They cannot be used directly as a litigation tool, nor do they automatically spawn implementing legislation (Levesque, 1996). With the current refractory climate towards the United Nations in the United States, it is unlikely that any future treaties will be ratified without reservations, or that reservations will be removed from existing treaties. However, even treaties ratified with significant reservations can still have an impact on social welfare in the United States. Most importantly, the ratification of a treaty signifies that a nation intends to comply with the overall spirit and intentions of that treaty. A treaty with reservations still holds power as a way for continued focus on an issue, as a lobbying tool, as an indirect litigation tool, and as a symbolic tool.

One of the most useful outcomes of ratifying a treaty is that a nation will then become subject to monitoring requirements, even if it does not consent to be adjudicated by the International Court of Justice. For example, the Convention on the Elimination on All Forms of Racial Discrimination requires an initial comprehensive report by all nations ratifying the treaty, and then subsequent reports every two years detailing the legislative, judicial, administrative, or other measures which they have adopted related to the provisions of the CERD (United Nations General Assembly, 1969, article 9). The United States, which ratified the CERD in 1994 with significant reservations rejecting adjudication by international courts, is still obligated to comply with this reporting requirement. The United States submitted its initial report in 2000, outlining in detail the history of racism in the United States, the progress towards eliminating racism, and the factors and barriers that currently affect full implementation of the CERD (U.S. State Department, 2000). This requirement enables the government to set clear goals related to the treaty issue, and to remain focused on these goals ensuring social welfare among its citizens (US Fund for UNICEF, 1998).

Treaties with reservations can also be used as a lobbying tool by domestic activists, as the United States would be required to abide by the spirit of the treaties even if it objected to particular issues within the treaty or enforcement procedures. As the environmental movement has come to realize, international policy guidelines can be a persuasive force in domestic policy formulation (Caldwell, 1990). The ratification of a treaty sets a precedent which can be influential among policymakers. Official policy actions, such as court rulings or legislative decisions, previously made by other levels or branches of the government, can also be useful precedents (Richan, 1991). Although referring to international policy recommendations does not guarantee success, it can help a lobbyist persuade legislators not only by showing that the United States has already committed to a certain principle by being party to an international agreement even with reservations, but also by illustrating the lobbyist's wide expertise about the policy, and by evoking a sense of international importance regarding the issue.

In a similar fashion, non-binding United Nations or OAS declarations, such as the UNUDHR, can also be used as lobbying tools.

Treaties with reservations can also be used *indirectly* as a litigation tool. While a treaty cannot be used as a specific protection of rights, both customary and conventional international laws are referred to frequently in the courts as tools for interpreting domestic statutes (Lillich, 1985). Finally, a treaty with significant reservations can still have some symbolic value both domestically and internationally. By becoming a party to a treaty, the United States sends a message that it at least agrees with the general principles underlying a treaty, and can participate in monitoring activities. However, the moral authority of the United States is greatly diminished when it refuses to subject itself to international litigation.

Impact of Treaties Not Ratified

Even if an international treaty is not ratified at all or is not designed to be legally binding, policymakers, practitioners, and activists within the United States can still borrow policy goals and ideas from these treaties, adapting the content of the treaties for either policy or practice. For example, even if the United States never ratifies the CRC, framing children's issues in terms of rights, with the best interest of the child as the primary factor, can be a useful concept borrowed from international treaties. While an unratified treaty does not carry the weight of federal law, this does not stop state and federal legislators from using this treaty as a guideline or justification for the passage of local or federal policy. For example, the rights outlined in the Declaration on the Rights of Mentally Retarded Persons, while not legally binding, could have served as a guide for state policy makers when developing initial disability protections.

The lack of treaty ratification also does not stop activists from referring to specific rights outlined in a treaty to promote social rights within the United States. For example, a letter to the editor condemning a New York proposal to imprison youths in adult prisons gained teeth when it claimed that if such a proposal "becomes law, New York would be flagrantly violating Articles 37 and 40 of the Convention on the Rights of the Child," (Beyer, 1995). Borrowing concepts from international treaties gives the concepts an initial level of legitimacy—particularly if a treaty has been widely ratified. However, as there has recently been a growing distrust of international agreements and the United Nations among some people in the United States, the use of international precedent may not have as much sway for these individuals.

In addition, even if the United States does not ratify a treaty, the national debate surrounding the ratification of a treaty can itself draw attention to the issues represented. For example, the process of fighting for the ratification of the CRC in the United States has led to several hundred news articles across the country, which highlights the issue of children's rights (LEXIS search, 2000), even if the treaty is never ratified.

Finally, even if a treaty is not officially ratified by the United States, if it does become a widely accepted practice by a number of countries, it will eventually become international customary law which can be legally binding on the United States. The UDHR is the prime example of a non-binding international agreement that has become binding through customary law, and it is likely that widely ratified treaties, such as the CRC, will eventually gain the same status.

References

Beyer, D. (1995, December 16). Domestic poverty is a human rights issue; protecting children [Letter to the editor]. *New York Times*, p. 22.

Caldwell, L. (1990). *International environmental policy: Emergence and dimensions*. Durham: Duke University Press.

Council of Europe. (1950). *Convention for the Protection of Human Rights and Fundamental Freedoms* (Rome, 4.XI.1950). Rome: Author.

Driscoll, D. (1989). The development of human rights in international law. In W. Lacquer, & B. Rubin (Eds.) *The human rights reader: Rev. ed.* New York: Penguin.

Eisenberg, M. (1988). The rights of people with disabilities to a barrier-free environment: U.S. compliance with international law. *International Law and Politics, 20*, 929–966.

Hall, K. (1993). *International human rights law: A resource guide*. Queenstown, MD: Aspen Institute.

Henkin, L. (1995). Comment: U.S. ratification of human rights conventions: The ghost of Senator Bricker. *The American Journal of International Law, 89*, 341+. Retrieved November 22, 2000, from LEXIS-NEXIS on-line database, 89 A.J.I.L. 341.

Hillier, T. (1994). Public international law. London: Cavendish.

Horowitz, D. (1999, November 26). Perspective on foreign policy; Even standing alone, the United States can still be right; The collectivist view undermines the U.S. constitutional tradition of individual. *Los Angeles Times*, B9. Retrieved November 22, 2000, from LEXIS-NEXIS on-line database.

Kilbourne, S. (1996). U.S. failure to ratify the U.N. Convention on the Rights of the Child: Playing politics with children's rights. *Transnational Law & Contemporary Problems, 6*, 437. Retrieved November 22, 2000, from LEXIS-NEXIS on-line database (6 Transnat'l L. & Contemp. Probs. 437).

Korr, W., Fallon, B., & Brieland, D. (1994). UN Convention on the Rights of the Child: implications for social work education. *International Social Work, 37*(4): 333–345.

Levesque, R. (1996). Future visions of juvenile justice: Lessons from international and comparative law. *Creighton Law Review, 29*, 1563–1585.

Lillich, R. (1985). Invoking international human rights law in domestic courts. *University of Cincinnati Law Review, 54*, 367. Retrieved November 28, 2000, from LEXIS-NEXIS on-line database (54 U. Cin. L. Rev. 367).

National Association of Social Workers. (1999). Code of ethics. National Association of Social Workers. Washington: Author. Retrieved November 25, 2000, from http://www.naswdc.org/Code/ethics.htm.

Nyland, B. (1999). The United Nations Convention on the Rights of the Child: Using a concept of rights as a basis for practice. *Australian Journal of Early Childhood, 24*(1), 9–15.

Richan, W. (1991). *Lobbying for social change.* New York: Haworth.

S. Res. 133, 104th Cong., 1st Sess, , 141 Cong Rec. S8400 (1995)

Schrijver, N. (1988). The role of the United Nations in the development of international law. In J. Harrod, & N. Schrijver (Eds.) *The UN Under Attack*. 33–56 Brookfield: Gower.

Stork, J. (1999). Human rights and U.S. policy. *In Focus, 4*(8). Retrieved November 25, 2000, from http://www.foreignpolicy-infocus.org/briefs/vol4/v4n08hrts.html.

United Nations. (1945). United Nations Charter (June 26, 1945, 59 Stat. 1031, T.X. 993, 3 Bevans 1153). New York: Author.

United Nations. (1999). United Nations treaty collection treaty reference guide. New York: United Nations. Retrieved November 27, 2000, from http://untreaty.un.org/.

United Nations Department of Public Information. (1987a). *Human rights questions and answers.* New York: The United Nations.

United Nations Department of Public Information. (1987b). *Basic facts about the United Nations.* New York: The United Nations.

United Nations General Assembly. (1948). *Universal declaration of human rights* (U.N. Document/A/810 at 71). New York: Author.

United Nations General Assembly. (1969). *International convention on the elimination of all forms of racial discrimination* (660 U.N.T.S. 195). New York: Author.

United Nations General Assembly. (1979). *Convention on the elimination of all forms of discrimination against women* (U.N. Document/A/34/46). New York: Author.

United Nations General Assembly. (1989). *Convention on the rights of the child.* (U.N. Document/A/Res/44/23). New York: Author.

United Nations General Assembly. (2000). *Women 2000: Gender equality, development and peace for the Twenty-first Century* [United Nations Department of Information DPI/2035/N-May 2000] New York: Author. Retrieved November 27, 2000, from http://www.un.org/womenwatch/daw/followup/session/presskit/gasp.htm

UNICEF. (1996). *The state of the world's children: 1996.* New York: Author.

U.S. Fund for UNICEF. (1998). *The rights of the child and other issues.* New York: Author. Retrieved on November 20, 2000, from http://www.unicefusa.org/infoactiv/rights.html.

U.S. State Department, Bureau of Democracy, Human Rights and Labor. 2000. *Initial report of the United States of America to the United Nations Committee on the Elimination of Racial Discrimination.* Washington, C: Author. Retrieved November 27, 2000, from http://www.state.gov/www/global/human_rights/cerd_report/cerd_toc.html.

Wittenberg, E. & Wittenberg, E. (1989). *How to win in Washington: Very practical advice about lobbying the grassroots and the media.* Cambridge: Blackwell.

Index

Addams, Jane, 4
Africa, 124–125, 128
Age discrimination, 15
Aged. *See* Elderly
Aging workforce and labor market
    policy, 14–16
    "good practice," 16
Aid to Families with Dependent
    Children (AFDC), 78
American Convention On Human
    Rights, 143–144

Barth, R. P., 37
Beveridge report of 1942, 64
Britain, 6–7, 41
    elderly suicide, 26
    social insurance system in,
        63–68
Bush, George W., 56–58

Canada, 35, 41, 43, 101–102
Capitalism, 110
Central Provident Fund (CPF), 61–63
Child abuse, 44–45

Child welfare, 31–32, 39–40, 47–48.
    See also Convention on the Rights
    of the Child; Family
    defined, 31
    and human capital, 121–123,
        127–128
    innovations borrowed, 32–33
    innovative programs from U.S.,
        40–43
    literature on, 33
    what U.S. can learn from other
        countries, 43–47
Childcare, 19–20, 46
Chile, social insurance system in,
    58–61, 67–70
China, 111
Community development and social
    capital, 6, 124–125, 128–130
Community Development Corpora-
    tions (CDCs), 129
Community living, 42
Community rights, 145
Community services, 38, 114
Community violence and PTSD, 97–99

Convention on the Elimination of All Forms of Discrimination against Women (CEDAW), 145, 147–148, 153
Convention on the Rights of the Child (CRC), 44, 145–147, 150, 152
Cooperatives, 126
Corporal punishment, 44–45

de Soto, Hernando, 110
Demonstration projects, 7
Denmark, 37, 76–77
Depression, 95–96
    Eastern *vs.* Western perspectives on, 96–97
Desjarlais, R., 93, 97
Development without Mobilization, 108
Development without the Achievable, 107
Development without the Poor, 107
Domestic violence. *See* Women, battering of

Earned Income Tax Credit (EITC), 85
East Germany, 22
Eastern cultures, mental illness in, 94, 96–97
Elder suicide, 24–26
Elderly population, 13–14, 26–27. *See also* Aging workforce
    long-term care, 21–24
Employment. *See* Aging workforce; Mental health, and the workplace; Microenterprise; Welfare
Empowerment theory, 40, 42, 43
English common law, 41. *See also* Britain
Europe. *See also under* Welfare
    aging societies, workforce, and pension reform, 17–19
European Convention on Human Rights and Fundamental Rights (ECHR), 143
European Union (EU), 17–18

Family care, shared, 37–38
Family/child practice, 33. *See also* Child welfare
Family group conferencing, 35–37
Family preservation services, 40–43
Family unity meeting, 35–36, 43
"Family values," 46–47
Female-headed households, 105
Feminism, 40
Foster care. *See* Family care, shared relative. *See* Kinship care
Foundation for International Assistance (FINCA), 131
France, 77–78

Germany
    long-term care assistance, 21–24
    pension reform, 20–21
Gil, David, 45
Global interdependence, 1–2
Globalization, 1, 3
Gore, Al, 57
Grameen Bank, 5, 6, 108–109, 126

Haifa Women's Coalition, 102–103
Head Start, 127–128
Healthy Start, 43
Hokenstad, M. C., 2, 6
Homelessness, 105
Hospice movement, 5
Human rights. *See also* Convention on the Rights of the Child; Rights treaties. *See also* International law and social welfare
    ratified by U.S., 147–151
    self-executing *vs.* non-self-executing, 149, 152

India, 123, 127, 128
Individual retirement accounts (IRAs), 53–56. *See also* Social security privatization and, 67–70
Information age, 3, 4
Integrated Child Welfare Services Scheme, 123, 127, 128

International Covenant on Civil and Political Rights (ICESCR), 140, 145
International Covenant on Economic, Social and Cultural Rights (ICESCR), 140, 145
International exchanges in social work, ix–x, 1–3
   models from other countries, 3–6
   recent projects and future opportunities, 6–8
International law and social welfare, 137–139
   generation of rights, 144–145
   impact of ratified treaties with significant reservations, 152–154
   impact of ratified treaties without reservations, 151–152
   impact of treaties not ratified, 154–155
   influence of treaties on U.S., 148
      ratification rights, 148–151
   international agreements
      general, 140, 141
      potential impacts, 151
      regional, 141, 143–144
      specialized, 140–143
   sample treaties, 145
Israel, domestic violence in, 102–103
Issues in International Social Work (Hokenstad & Midgley), x, 3
Italy, 112

Kinship care, 33–35
   state-funded, 34–35

Loans, 5–6. *See also* Microenterprise
Local Initiative Support Corporation (LISC), 129

Machiavelli, Nicolò, 106
Medical innovations, 7–8

Mental health, 93, 114. *See also specific topics*
   Internet as international resource, 113–114
   lessons from abroad, 93–95
   poverty and, 105–107
   social and economic development and, 107–110
   and the workplace, 110–113
Mental well-being, categories of experience that promote, 113
Microenterprise and social assistance, 6, 125–126, 130–131
Midgley, James, 2, 119
Moreno, J. L., 98–99
Mothers, single, 105

Neighborhood-based interagency teams, 38
Netherlands, 77
New Zealand, child welfare in, 34–36
9/11, 1–2
NOAM, 102

Organizations, international, 2–3

Pact of San Jose, 143–144
Parent education, 46
Patch Project, 38
Pecora, Peter, 37
Peer lending. *See* Grameen Bank
Pension crises, 17
Pension policy and reform, 16–21
Pension Reform 2000 bill (Germany), 20–21
Pensions. *See* Social security
Perkins, Frances, 4
Peru, 110
Pflegeversicherung, 21–24
Population aging, 13–14
Population growth, 13
Posttraumatic stress disorder (PTSD)
   and community violence, 97–99
   rape and, 103, 104

Poverty, 45, 46, 76. *See also* Welfare, poverty, and social services
  women in, 105–109
Privatization. *See* Social security
Profiles in International Social Work (NASW Press), x
Property registries and ownership, 110
Psychodrama, community trauma and, 98–99
PsychoSocial Spectrum model, 95–97

Queensland, Australia, 100, 101

Rape, 103–105
Refugees, 103–105
Restorative justice, 38–39
Retirement accounts. *See* Social security; individual retirement accounts
Retirement age, 14–15. *See also* Pension policy
Revenu Minimum d'Insertion (RMI) program, 81
Rights. *See also* Human rights; International law and social welfare
  first, second, and third generation, 144–145

Schizophrenics Anonymous, 113–114
Self-employment, productive, 125
Singapore, social security in, 61–63, 68–69
Social and economic development, 107–110, 117–119. *See also* Mental health
Social assistance and microenterprise, 6, 125–126, 130–131
Social capital, 124
Social cooperatives, 112
Social development (approach), 118–119
  benefit of adapting, 131–133
  in Global South, 117–119, 121–126
  historical evolution, 119–120
  productivist social welfare, 120–121
  promoted in U.S., 126–131

Social firms, 111–112
Social inclusion *vs.* exclusion, 75–76
Social insurance, 4–5, 54–55, 58, 64
Social investment policies and programs, 119
Social security, 5, 53–55. *See also* Pension policy
  Bush proposals, 56–58
  international experiences, 58–67
Social welfare policy. *See also* Welfare
  models of, 4–5
Social work education, 2
Social work organizations, 2–3
Stanton, Elizabeth Cady, 106
State Earnings-Related Pension Scheme (SERPS), 64–66
Strengthening Families through International Innovations Transfer, 6, 37
Strengths perspective, 43
Sweden, 78
  pension policy, 19–21

Tax incentives, 65–66
Telecommunications technology, 3, 4
Temporary Assistance for Needy Families (TANF), 78–79
Train the Trainers model, 109–110
Treaties. *See* International law and social welfare

United Nations High Commissioner of Refugees (UNHCR), 103, 104
United Nations International Children's Emergency Fund (UNICEF), 107–108, 140

van Wormer, K., 105–106
Voluntary agencies, 4

Welfare, poverty, and social services, 45, 75–76
  contracts and incentives, 80–82
  European experiences, 76–78
  experience of U.S., 78–80
  lessons from abroad, 87–89
  policy questions, 82–87

Women
    battering of, 99–100
        attention to male
          batterers, 100–103
    oppression of, 103–107, 145,
      147–148, 153
    in poverty, 105–109
    shelters for, 100–102

Work Opportunity Reconciliation Act
    of 1996, 78
Working Capital, 130–131
World Bank, 109
World Health Organization (WHO),
    103, 104

Yunus, Muhammad, 108

About the Editors

M.C. Hokenstad, PhD, is the Ralph S. and Dorothy P. Schmitt Professor in the Mandel School of Applied Social Sciences and professor of International Health in the School of Medicine at Case Western Reserve University. He has long been active in international organizations and currently serves as membership secretary of the International Association of Schools of Social Work and as a member of the United Nations Non-Governmental Committee on Aging. Dr. Hokenstad has been editor-in-chief of the *International Social Work Journal* and has published extensively in the fields of international social welfare, social gerontology, and social work education. His books include *Participation in Teaching and Learning: An Idea Book for Social Work Educators* (with Barry Rubgy, 1977), *Linking Health Care and Social Services* (with Roger Rituo, 1982), *Gerontological Social Work: International Perspectives* (with Katherine Kendall, 1988), *Profiles in International Social Work* (with James Midgley and S.K. Khinduka, 1992), and *Issues in International Social Work: Global Challenges for a New Century* (with James Midgley, 1997). He has received two Fulbright Awards for teaching and research in Scandinavia and has been a visiting professor and program consultant at several universities in Europe and Asia.

James Midgley, PhD, is the Harry and Riva Specht Professor of Public Social Services and dean of the School of Social Welfare at the University of California at Berkeley. He has published widely on international social work, social development, and social policy. His major books include *Professional Imperialism: Social Work in the Third World* (1961); *Social Security, Inequality, and the Third World* (1984), *Comparative Social Policy and the Third World* (with Stewart MacPherson, 1987), *Profiles in International Social Work* (with M.C. Hokenstad and S.K. Khinduka, 1992), *Social Development: The Development Perspective in Social Welfare* (1995), *Social Welfare in Global Context* (1997), and *Issues in International Social Work: Global Challenges for a New Century* (with M.C. Hokenstad, 1997). He has also contributed to many leading social policy, social work, and development journal studies.

MORE RESOURCES ON INTERNATIONAL SOCIAL WORK

Lessons from Abroad: *Adapting International Social Welfare Innovations,* by M.C. Hokenstad and James Midgley, Editors. Regarded as among the world's leaders in formulating social work policy and practice, U.S. social workers have much to learn from colleagues in other nations. The third in an NASW Press series on international social work, this book examines how domestic policies and practice can be enhanced by documenting, analyzing and judiciously adapting innovative approaches emanating from other countries.

ISBN: 0-87101-360-6. 2004. Item #3606. $44.99.

Issues in International Social Work: *Global Challenges for a New Century,* M.C. Hokenstad and James Midgley, Editors. *Issues in International Social Work* provides a concise briefing on the critical issues in international social work at the beginning of the 21st century. It examines the place of social work in a global economy, the contribution of social work to social development, the role of social workers in addressing ethnic conflicts, the direction of social work in response to new international needs, and more.

ISBN: 0-87101-280-4. Item #2804. $26.95.

School Social Work Worldwide, *Marion Huxtable and Eric Blyth, Editors. School Social Work Worldwide* opens the boundaries of international school social work as never before. Leaders in the field from 12 countries provide eye-opening perspectives and innovative interventions that make a compelling statement about the value of learning from one another to ensure that the world's children reach their full potential through education. Sequentially arranged chapters follow the expansion of school social work around the world and then look ahead to policy and practice issues for the future.

ISBN: 0-87101-348-7. January 2002. Item #3487. $44.99.

Faithful Angels: *Portraits of International Social Work Notables,* James O. Billups, Editor. *Faithful Angels* is a collection of in-depth personal interviews with 15 notable social work leaders from 13 countries. The book illustrates how these social workers have helped advance social work, social development, and human realization in their own societies, across national boundaries, and, in many instances, around the globe. It is a unique and inspiring book that presents for the first time a modern-day historical record of international social work professionals.

ISBN: 0-87101-349-5. Item #3495. $34.99.

The Global Crisis of Violence: *Common Problems, Universal Causes, Shared Solutions,* by Dorothy Van Soest. This eye-opening book sets forth the concepts of violence in systemic terms in the context of culture and institution. It examines the connections between development and violence in areas such as poverty, gender violence, violence against children, and ethnoviolence, and presents effective strategies to address the causes and impacts of violence worldwide. An important text for policy courses and for courses in human behavior in the social environment.

ISBN: 0-87101-276-6. Item #2766. $35.95.

Challenges of Violence Worldwide: *A Curriculum Module, An Educational Resource,* produced by the *Violence & Development Project.* The student guide, *An Educational Resource,* focuses on violence as a global affliction and on sustainable human development as a global antidote. Faculty will use the accompanying *Curriculum Module* to develop and teach this important content, which meets the CSWE accreditation standards for effective education programs that recognize the interdependence of nations. Using these materials, students will gain a broad understanding of violence and the social work role in conflict resolution on a global scale.

Educational Resource—ISBN: 0-87101-269-3. Item #2693. $16.95.
Curriculum Module—ISBN: 0-87101-268-5. Item #2685. $20.95.

(Order form and information on reverse side)

ORDER FORM

Qty.	Title	Item #	Price	Total
___	Lessons from Abroad	3606	$44.99	_____
___	Issues in International Social Work	2804	$26.95	_____
___	School Social Work Worldwide	3487	$44.99	_____
___	Faithful Angels	3495	$34.99	_____
___	The Global Crisis of Violence	2766	$35.95	_____
Challenges of Violence Worldwide				
____	Educational Resource	2693	$16.95	_____
____	Curriculum Module	2685	$20.95	_____

Subtotal	_____
Postage and Handling	_____
DC residents add 6% sales tax	_____
MD residents add 5% sales tax	_____
NC residents add 4.5% sales tax	_____
Total	_____

POSTAGE AND HANDLING
Minimum postage and handling fee is $4.95. Orders that do not include appropriate postage and handling will be returned.

DOMESTIC: Please add 12% to orders under $100 for postage and handling. For orders over $100 add 7% of order.

CANADA: Please add 17% postage and handling.

OTHER INTERNATIONAL: Please add 22% postage and handling.

❒ **Check** or **money order** (payable to NASW Press) for $ _____.

❒ **Credit card**
   ❒ Visa ❒ MasterCard ❒ American Express

_____   _____
Credit Card Number   Expiration Date

Signature _____

Name_____

Address _____

City _____ State/Province _____

Country _____ Zip _____

Phone _____ E-mail _____

NASW Member # (if applicable) _____

(Please make checks payable to NASW Press. Prices are subject to change.)

NASW PRESS
P. O. Box 431
Annapolis JCT, MD 20701
USA

Credit card orders call
1-800-227-3590
(In the Metro Wash., DC, area, call 301-317-8688)
Or fax your order to 301-206-7989
Or order online at www.naswpress.org

CPLA04